Beginning Folk Guitar

By Jerry Silverman

OAK PUBLICATIONS

New York · London · Sydney · Cologne

Cover photo of Nick Seeger by Herbert Wise.

Singer, songwriter, Nick Seeger, was born in Ithaca, New
York, raised in Holland, and presently lives in Hopewell
Junction, New York. Since the release of his first album,
Sail On Flying Dutchman, on the Biograph label, he has
done several tours of Europe, Canada, Alaska, and regularly
tours the U.S. performing at colleges, and folk and bluegrass
festivals.

Original drawings and diagrams by Jim Infantino
Music and tablature copy by Igon Puchalski
Documentary illustrations selected and positioned by Moses Asch
Layout and production by Jean Hammons

International Standard Book Number: 0-8256-0015-0

Distributed throughout the world by Music Sales Corporation:

33 West 60th Street, New York 10023
78 Newman Street, London W1P 3LA
27 Clarendon Street, Artarmon, Sydney NSW 2064
Kölner Strasse 199, D-5000, Cologne 90

CONTENTS

JERRY SILVERMAN is one of the foremost folk-guitar
instructors in America. His published and recorded works
have made an important contribution to the appreciation
and study of folk music and folk styles.

Also by Jerry Silverman:

Books
*The Art of The Folk Blues Guitar (Oak)
*The Flat-Picker's Guitar Guide (Oak)
 Folk Blues (Oak/Macmillan)
 The Folksinger's Guide To Chords and Tunings (Oak)
 The Folksinger's Guide to Note Reading and Music Theory (Oak)
*The Folksinger's Guitar Guide, Vol. 1 (Oak)
*The Folksinger's Guitar Guide, Vol. 2 (Oak)
 A Russian Song Book (Random House) - Music Editor - and Translator
 Russian Songs (Oak)
 62 Outrageous Songs (Oak)
 Songs of the Civil War (Columbia University Press) - Music Editor.

*Also available in Oak Record Editions.

INTRODUCTION

The needs of the beginning folk guitarist are twofold:

1. Basic information and direction as to chords and various techniques of playing.
2. Extensive folk song material upon which to practice and develop these techniques.

Whereas most folk guitar instruction books cover point "one" to a greater or lesser extent, point "two" is generally skimped over in an effort to "conserve space". This leaves the bewildered beginner on his own too soon in his search for a technique-building repertoire. It is the intent here to go into much greater detail and to procede much more slowly with the crucial first stages of study so that the student may emerge from his first few months with the guitar with a solid foundation of basic techniques.

INSTRUCTION RECORD

In order to aid the student in the learning of the material in this book I have prepared an instruction record (Beginning The Folk Guitar, Folkways FS8353) containing illustrative material taken from each of the chapters of this book.

HOW TO HOLD THE GUITAR

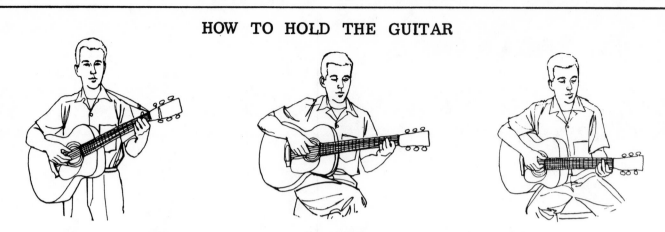

The two most commonly used types of guitar for folksong accompaniment.
See page 94 for a discussion of the relative merits of these instruments.

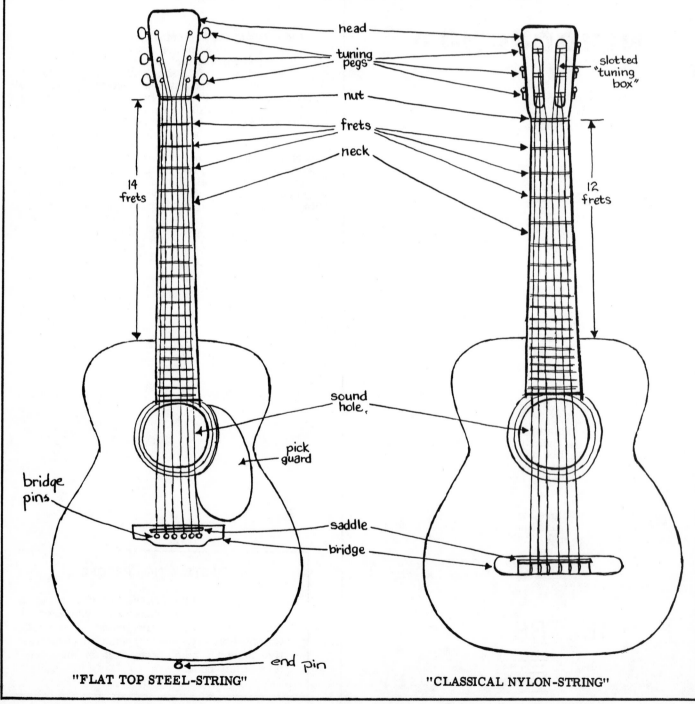

head

tuning pegs

slotted "tuning box"

nut

frets

neck

14 frets

12 frets

sound hole

pick guard

bridge pins

saddle

bridge

end pin

"FLAT TOP STEEL-STRING"

"CLASSICAL NYLON-STRING"

I. TABLATURE

Tablature is a time-honored system of music notation which shows the player of a particular instrument which string and fret to pluck, which hole to cover or which key to press rather than the actual note on the musical staff.

In guitar tablature we use six lines to represent the six strings of the instrument as follows:

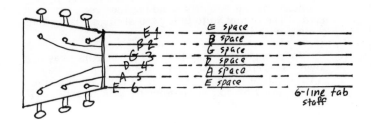

Numbers above each line (in the spaces) will indicate at what fret the string is to be pressed to the fingerboard by a finger of the left hand. Thus, if you played a scale starting on the lowest string (E-major scale.)

tablature would show it in this manner:

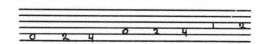

MELTAB and GITAB

MELTAB is the tablature which indicates where the actual notes of the melody of the piece being sung may be played. It will be written directly below the melody line. By the use of MELTAB it will be possible to play the tunes of unfamiliar songs - thereby learning them.

GITAB is the tablature for the guitar part. GITAB and the guitar part itself will be written out only when there is a specific need to illustrate some technical point. Experience has shown that it is unnecessary and confusing to write out measure after measure of a repetitive strum when merely describing it once would suffice.

 = MELTAB

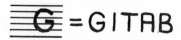 = GITAB

THE OPENER OF THE TRAIL

II. CHORD DIAGRAMS and CHORDS

For the notation of chords we shall use the standard "chord diagram" as well as the musical notation and the tablature for each chord. The diagram is an "aerial view" of the fingerboard of the guitar.

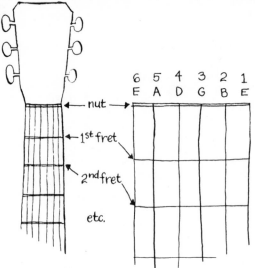

Now we will learn our first two chords.

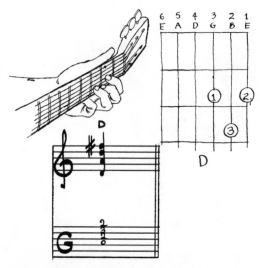

play strings 4, 3, 2, 1

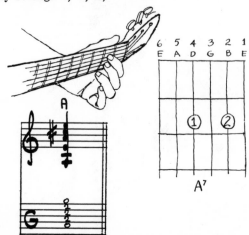

play strings 5, 4, 3, 2, 1

The numbers in the circles represent the fingers of the left hand. Make sure that the fingernails of this hand are trimmed as closely as possible. You have to press almost <u>straight down</u> on the strings to avoid accidentally touching more than one string at a time. Long fingernails would make this finger position difficult if not impossible.

Place the fingers of the left hand as close to the higher numbered fret (as shown in the diagram) as possible without actually touching the fret. Press down hard. The object is to bring the strings firmly into contact with the proper frets.

Your fingertips may become sore from pressing down the strings. The best thing to do in the beginning is to practice for short periods of time - but often. After a week or so the tenderness will disappear (if the fingers haven't done so first).

NOTE how easy it is to change from D to A_7 and from A_7 to D. The first and second fingers move as a unit (more or less) from strings three and one (for D) to four and two (for A_7). The third finger just pops up and down at the right time... Easy?

You can play dozens of songs using the D and A_7 chords.

WARNING: Do not play on each syllable of every word. Rather start strumming with a slow, steady, evenly <u>pulsed</u> beat and sing the words "rhythmically" over the accompaniment.

RIGHT HAND: Let your nails grow somewhat longer on your right hand. You'll need them a little later for some of the strums we're going to learn.

HUSH LITTLE BABY

HUSH, LIT-TLE BA-BY, DON'T SAY A WORD

POP-PA'S GON-NA BUY YOU A MOCK-ING-BIRD,

IF THAT MOCK-ING-BIRD DON'T SING

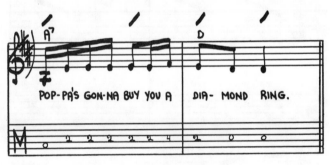

POP-PA'S GON-NA BUY YOU A DIA-MOND RING.

D   A7
And if that diamond ring is brass,
             D
Papa's gonna buy you a looking-glass,
           A7
And if that looking-glass gets broke,
            D
Papa's gonna buy you a billy goat.

And if that billy goat don't pull,
Papa's gonna buy you a cart and bull.
And if that cart and bull turn over,
Papa's gonna buy you a dog named Rover.

And if that dog named Rover don't bark,
Papa's gonna buy you a horse and cart.
And if that horse and cart fall down,
You'll still be the sweetest little baby in town.

9

III. BASS-CHORD THUMB STRUM

Now take the D chord and just pluck the fourth string with the thumb of your right hand. Then brush down across the rest (3rd, 2nd, 1st) of the strings.

Now try the same thing with the A_7 chord. Only this time pluck the fifth string with your thumb and brush down over the first four strings.

Try it over and over until it comes easy.

Now we're ready to try some songs with the D and A_7 chords played in this "oom-pah" manner.

Always start strumming the first chord before you start singing. This "introduction" will give you the pitch of the first note and help get you "in the mood".

PUTTING ON THE STYLE

CRACKS HIS WHIP SO LIVE-LY, JUST TO SEE HIS LA-DY

VE-RY APT TO SMILE, TO SEE SO MA-NY

SMILE, BUT SHE KNOWS HE'S ON-LY

PEO-PLE PUT-TING ON THE STYLE.

Chorus

PUT-TING ON THE STYLE. PUT-TING ON THE

A-GO-NY, PUT-TING ON THE STYLE,

THAT'S WHAT ALL THE YOUNG FOLKS ARE DO-ING ALL THE

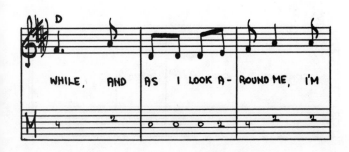

WHILE, AND AS I LOOK A-ROUND ME, I'M

D
Sweet sixteen and goes to Church
           A7
Just to see the boys;

Laughs and giggles
      D
At every little noise.

She turns this way a little,
           A7
Then turns that way a while,

But everybody knows she's only
        D
Putting on the style.

Chorus

Young man in a restaurant
Smokes a dirty pipe;
Looking like a pumpkin
That's only half-way ripe.
Smoking, drinking, chewing --
And thinking all the while
That there is nothing equal
To putting on the style.

Chorus

Preacher in the pulpit
Shouting with all his might,
Glory Hallelujah --
Put the people in a fright.
You might think that Satan's
Coming up the aisle,
But it's only the preacher
Putting on the style.

Chorus

Young man just from college
Makes a big display
With a great big jawbreak
Which he can hardly say;
It can't be found in Webster's
And won't be for a while,
But everybody knows he's only
Putting on the style.

Chorus

GYPSY DAVY

IT WAS

Start singing on "and"

COUNT: ONE - AND TWO - AND   ONE - AND TWO - AND

LATE LAST NIGHT WHEN THE BOSS CAME HOME A-

ONE - AND TWO - AND   ONE - AND TWO - AND

ASK- ING FOR HIS LA- DY. THE

ON- LY AN- SWER_ HE RE- CEIVED, "SHE'S

GONE WITH THE GYP- SY DA— VY, SHE'S

GONE WITH THE GYP- SY DAVE."

12

D
Go saddle for me my buckskin horse

And a hundred-dollar saddle.

Point out to me their wagon tracks
    A7   D
And after them I'll travel,
  A7   D
After them I'll ride.

Well I had not rode to the midnight
    moon
When I saw the campfire gleaming.
I heard the notes of the big guitar
And the voice of the Gypsies singing
That song of the Gypsy Dave.

There in the light of the camping fire,
I saw her fair face beaming.
Her heart in tune to the big guitar
And the voice of the Gypsies singing
That song of the Gypsy Dave.

Have you forsaken your house and home,
Have you forsaken your baby?
Have you forsaken your husband dear
To go with the Gypsy Davey,
And sing with the Gypsy Davey
That song of the Gypsy Dave? **

Yes I've forsaken my husband dear
To go with the Gypsy Davey,
And I've forsaken my mansion high
But not my blue-eyed baby,
Not my blue-eyed babe.

She smiled to leave her husband dear
And go with the Gypsy Davey;
But the tears come a-trickling down
    her cheeks
To think of the blue-eyed baby,
Pretty little blue-eyed babe.

Take off, take off your buckskin gloves
Made of Spanish leather;
Give to me your lily-white hand
And we'll ride home together,
We'll ride home again.

No, I won't take off my buckskin gloves,
They're made of Spanish leather.
I'll go my way from day to day
And sing with the Gypsy Davey,
That song of the Gypsy Davey,
That song of the Gypsy Davey,
That song of the Gypsy Dave, ***

** Repeat the last three measures to get it all in.
*** Repeat the last seven measures to get it all in.

GOOD NEWS

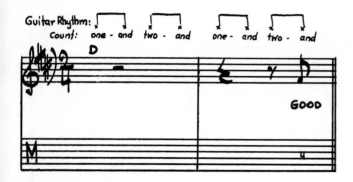

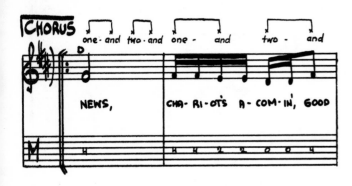

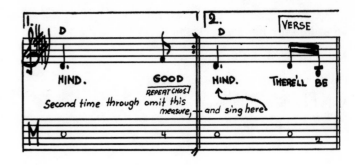

D
There's a long white robe in Heaven I know (3)
                  A7   D
And I don't want it to leave a-me behind.

There's a better land in this world I know...

Standard Chord Combinations

Chords are generally played in standard combinations with other chords. These combinations comprise what are known musically as "keys". We have been playing in the key of D (major). If we learn one other chord in the key of D we will literally be able to play thousands of songs. (See page 89 for an important discussion of these "standard" combinations.)

The third chord we need to know in the key of D is G.

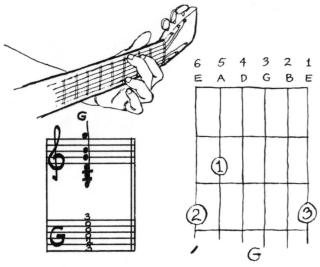

play all six strings

The thumb of the right hand strikes the 6th string and strums over the rest of the strings as with D and A7.

Play back and forth with these three chords until you know them so well that you can sing a song without thinking about them.

ATTENTION FINGERNAIL BITERS...

If you really must, then please direct your efforts to your left hand only...

THE BANKS OF THE OHIO

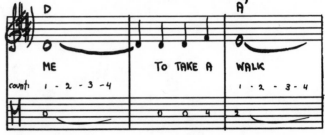

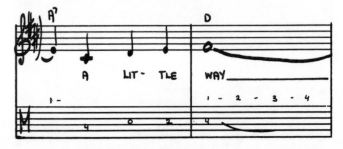

16

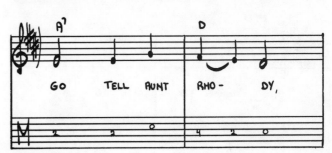

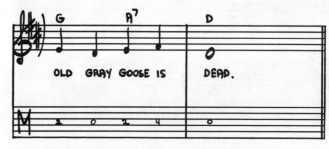

D   A7   D
Then only say that you'll be mine,
      A7   D
And in no other arms entwine,
                        G
Down beside where the waters flow,
      D   A7 D
Along the banks of the Ohio.

I asked your mother for you, dear,
And she said you were too young;
Only say that you'll be mine --
Happiness in my home you'll find.

Chorus

I held a knife against her breast,
And gently in my arms she pressed,
Crying: Willie, oh Willie, don't murder me,
For I'm unprepared for eternity.

Chorus

I took her by her lily white hand,
Led her down where the waters stand.
I picked her up and I pitched her in,
Watched her as she floated down.

Chorus

I started back home twixt twelve and
    one,
Crying, My God, what have I done?
I've murdered the only woman I love,
Because she would not be my bride.

D
The one that she's been a-saving,
     A7
The one that she's been a-saving,
D
The one that she's been a-saving
    G   A7   D
To make her a featherbed.

She died last Friday
    She died last Friday,
She died last Friday
    Behind the old barn shed.

She left nine little goslins,
    She left nine little goslins,
She left nine little goslins
    To scratch for their own bread.

OLEANNA

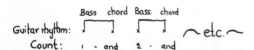

OH, TO BE IN O-LE-AN-NA

THAT'S WHERE I'D LIKE TO BE,

THAN BE BOUND IN NOR-WAY AND

DRAG THE CHAINS OF SLAV-ER-Y.

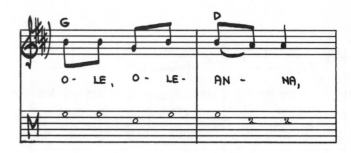

O - LE, O - LE - AN - NA,

O - LE, O - LE, O - LE, O - LE,

O - LE, O - LE - AN - NA.

Chorus

O - LE, O - LE, AN - NA,

D   G   D
In Oleanna land is free; the wheat and corn just plant

  themselves.
  A7   D   A7
Then grow a good four feet a day, while on your bed
     D
you rest yourself.

Chorus

Beer as sweet as Munchener springs from the
  ground and flows away.
The cows all like to milk themselves and hens lay
  eggs ten times a day.

Chorus

Little roasted piggies rush about the city streets,
Inquiring so politely if a slice of ham you'd like to eat.

Chorus

Say, if you'd begin to live, to Oleana you must go.
The poorest wretch in Norway becomes a duke in
  a year or so.

KEY OF A MAJOR

I and V₇ Chords

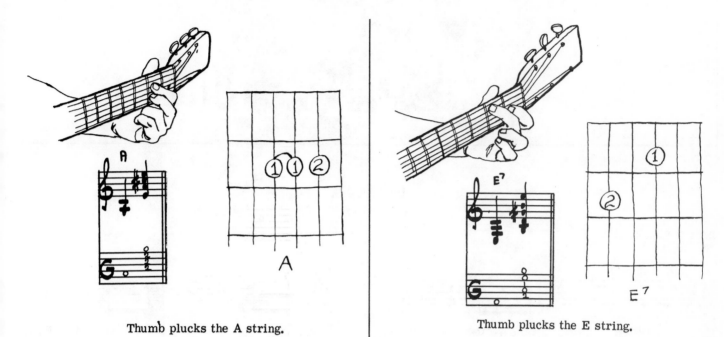

Thumb plucks the A string.

Thumb plucks the E string.

The third chord in the key of A is D, which you
already know.

GREEN CORN

Chorus

GREEN CORN, COME A- LONG CHAR- LIE,

GREEN CORN, DON'T-CHA TELL POL- LY,

GREEN CORN, COME A- LONG CHAR- LIE,

GREEN CORN, DONT-CHA TELL POL- LY.

Verse

ALL I WANT IN THIS CRE - A - TION,

PRET-TY LIT-TLE WIFE AND A BIG PLAN- TA - TION.

A
All I need to make me happy,
E7
Two little kids to call me pappy.

Chorus

One named Bill, the other named Davy,
They like their biscuits slopped in
    gravy.

All I need in this creation,
Three months work and nine vacation.

Chorus

Tell my boss any old time,
Daytime's his but nighttime's mine.

Chorus

BILE THEM CABBAGE DOWN

Chorus

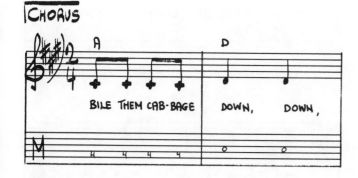

BILE THEM CAB-BAGE DOWN, DOWN,

TURN THEM HOE-CAKES 'ROUND, THE

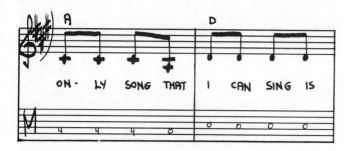

ON-LY SONG THAT I CAN SING IS

BILE THEM CAB-BAGE DOWN.

Verse

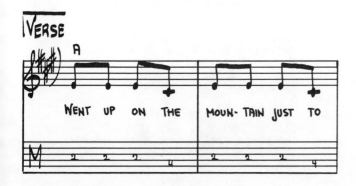

WENT UP ON THE MOUN-TAIN JUST TO

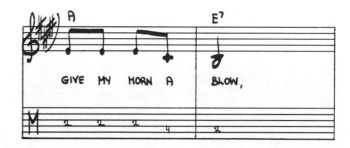

GIVE MY HORN A BLOW,

THOUGHT I HEARD MY TRUE LOVE SAY,

"YON-DER COMES MY BEAU."

A
Took my gal to the blacksmith shop
                E7
To have her mouth made small
  A   D
She turned around a time or two
  A   E7   A
And swallowed shop and all.

Possum in a 'simmon tree,
Raccoon on the ground,
Raccoon says, "You son-of-a-gun,
Shake some 'simmons down!"

Someone stole my old 'coon dog,
Wish they'd bring him back,
He chased the big hogs through the fence
And the little ones through the crack.

Met a possum in the road,
Blind as he could be,
Jumped the fence and whipped my dog
And bristled up at me.

Once I had an old gray mule,
His name was Simon Slick,
He'd roll his eyes and back his ears,
And how that mule would kick.

How that mule would kick!
He kicked with his dying breath;
He shoved his hind feet down his throat
And kicked himself to death.

OLD DAN TUCKER

WENT TO TOWN THE OTH-ER NIGHT TO

HEAR A NOISE AND SEE A FIGHT,

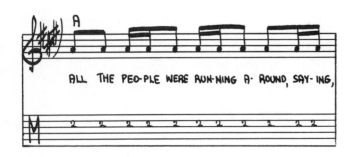

ALL THE PEO-PLE WERE RUN-NING A-ROUND, SAY-ING,

OLD DAN TUCK-ER'S COME TO TOWN.

CHORUS

GET OUT THE WAY, OLD DAN TUCK-ER,

YOU'RE TOO LATE TO COME FOR SUP-PER.

SUP-PER'S OV-ER AND DIN-NER'S COOK-ING AND

OLD DAN TUCK-ER JUST STAND-ING THERE LOOK-ING.

A
Old Dan Tucker's a fine old man,
E7
Washed his face in a frying pan.

A
Combed his hair with a wagon wheel,
E7   A
And died with a toothache in his heel.

Old Dan Tucker come to town,
Riding a billy goat, leading a hound.
Hound barked and the billygoat jumped,
Throwed old Dan right straddle of a stump.

Old Dan Tucker clumb a tree,
His Lord and Master for to see,
The limb it broke and Dan got a fall,
Never got to see his Lord at all.

Old Dan Tucker he got drunk,
Fell in the fire and he kicked up a chunk;
Red hot coal got in his shoe,
Lord Godamighty, how the ashes flew!

Old Dan Tucker he come to town,
Swinging the ladies 'round and 'round,
First to the right and then to the left,
And then to the one that you love the best.

IV. BASIC RIGHT-HAND FINGER STRUM

Before going on with the learning of new chords let's try something new with the right hand. Instead of just brushing your thumb down across the top three strings we will now employ the <u>fingers</u> of the right hand in plucking those strings. The <u>thumb</u> will now strike only the bass string of the chord. Place your fingers on the first three strings as follows:

First-(Index) finger on the third string
Second-(Middle) finger on the second string
Third-(Ring) finger on the first string

The thumb rests on either the E, A or D string depending on the chord. Keep the wrist womewhat arched and the thumb at right angles to the direction of movement of the fingers. (Sort of an inverted hitch-hiker's position.)

EXERCISE

1. With the fingers resting lightly on the proper strings strike the 6th string several times with the thumb. Do not move the fingers while moving the thumb.
2. With the thumb resting on the 6th string pluck the three strings gently by moving the fingers upward and inward as if clenching a fist (but not all the way - just enough to sound the strings). DON'T MOVE YOUR WRIST.
3. Now alternate - first the thumb then the fingers.
4. Play a few chords and see what it sounds like. That muffled sound you hear is probably a result of the fingers of your <u>left</u> hand not pressing down properly.
5. Be careful NOT TO BEND YOUR THUMB as you pluck the bass notes. Particularly important when playing a D chord; otherwise your thumb moving down will "bump into" your fingers moving up.

Try the songs you have already learned using this strum.

TWO MINOR CHORDS

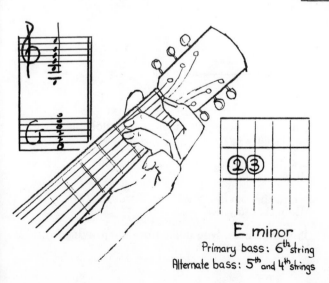

E minor
Primary bass: 6th string
Alternate bass: 5th and 4th strings

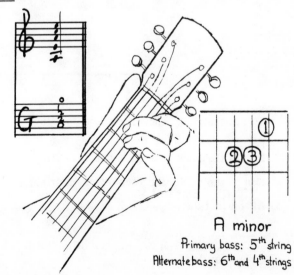

A minor
Primary bass: 5th string
Alternate bass: 6th and 4th strings

OH, SINNER MAN (I)

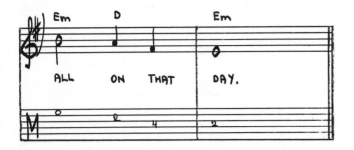

OH, SINNER MAN (II)

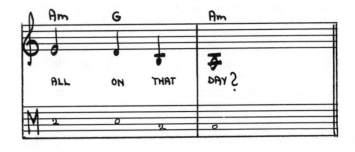

Em (Am)
Run to the rock, the rock was a-melting,

D(G)
Run to the rock, the rock was a-melting,
Em(Am)
Run to the rock, the rock was a-melting,
   D(G)   Em(Am)
All on that day.

Run to the sea, the sea was a-boiling (3),
All on that day.

Run to the moon, the moon was a-bleeding (3),
All on that day.

Run to the Lord, Lord won't you hide me? (3)
All on that day.

Run to the Devil, Devil was a-waiting (3),
All on that day.

Oh sinner man, you oughta been a-praying (3),
All on that day.

WHAT SHALL WE DO WITH THE DRUNKEN SAILOR (I)

WHAT SHALL WE DO WITH THE DRUNKEN SAILOR (II)

Put him in the scuppers with a hose pipe on him (3)...

Chorus

Heave him by the leg in a running bowline (3)...

Chorus

Shave his belly with a rusty razor (3)...

Chorus

That's what we'll do with the drunken sailor (3)...

Chorus

Chorus

Em(Am)
Hooray, and up she rises,
D(G)
Hooray, and up she rises,
Em(Am)
Hooray, and up she rises,
     D(G) Em(Am)
Earlye in the morning

V. THREE QUARTER ($\frac{3}{4}$) TIME

The songs that we have had up to now are in what is called duple meter (or duple time). That is the basic rhythmic feeling is either "one-two one-two", or "one-two-three-four", ($\frac{2}{4}$ or $\frac{4}{4}$) On the guitar, as you know these are played in an "oom-pah" alternation of bass-note and chord. Many songs, however are in triple meter or, most commonly, three-quarter time ($\frac{3}{4}$). Note: these time signatures are not fractions. It is not three divided by four but an indication that there are three (or two, or four) quarter notes in each measure. $\frac{3}{4}$ time is often referred to as "waltz time."

To play in $\frac{3}{4}$ time the most common practise is as follows:
First beat: THUMB plucks bass note
Second beat: FINGERS pluck up
Third beat: FINGERS pluck up

Count: <u>1</u> - 2 - 3 <u>1</u> - 2 - 3 <u>1</u> - 2 - 3

DOWN IN THE VALLEY

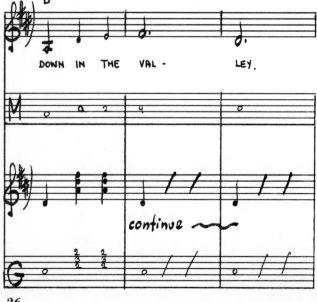

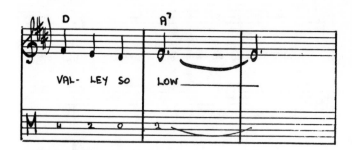

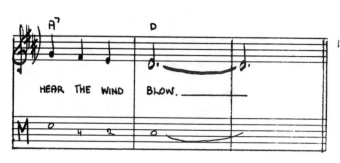

D   A7
Hear the wind blow, love, hear the wind blow,
                          D
Hang your head over, hear the wind blow.

If you don't love me, love whom you please.
Throw your arms 'round me give my heart ease.

Give my heart ease love, give my heart ease,
Throw your arms 'round me give my heart ease.

Write me a letter send it by mail,
Send it in care of the Birmingham Jail.

Birmingham Jail, love, Birmingham Jail,
Send it in care of the Birmingham Jail.

Build me a castle forty feet high,
So I can see her as she rides by.

As she rides by, love, as she rides by,
So I can see her as she rides by.

Roses love sunshine, violets love dew,
Angels in heaven know I love you.

Know I love you dear, know I love you,
Angels in heaven know I love you.

I NEVER WILL MARRY

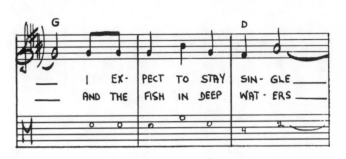

Chorus

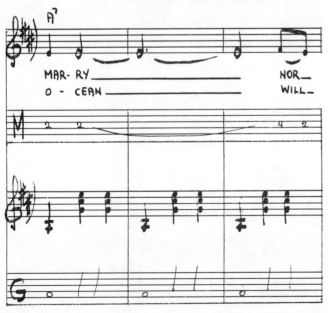

D   A7   G
One day as I rambled down by the seashore,
      D   A7   D
The wind it did whistle and the waters did roar.
   A7   D   G
I spied a fair damsel make a pitiful cry,
      D   A7   D
It sounded so lonesome in the waters nearby.

Chorus

My love's gone and left me,. he's the
  one I adore,
He's gone where I never shall see him
  any more.
She plunged her dear body, in the
  water so deep,
She closed her pretty blue eyes, in the
  waters to sleep.

Chorus

I WISH I WAS SINGLE AGAIN

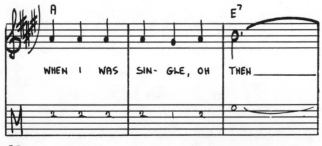

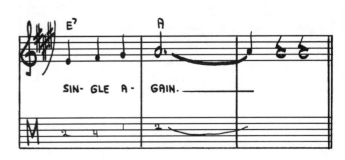

A
I married me a wife, oh then, oh then;
                             E7
I married me a wife, oh then.
 A   D
I married me a wife, she's the curse of my life,
   E7   A
And I wish I was single again.

My wife she died...
... and I laughed till I cried...

I went to the funeral...
... and danced Yankee Doodle...

I married another...
... the devil's grandmother...

She beat me, she banged me...
... I thought she would hang me...

She went for the rope...
... when she got it 'twas broke...

Young men, take warning from this...
Be good to the first, for the next is much worse...

28

VI. ALTERNATING BASS

Learning chords on the guitar is pretty much of a routine matter. You can look at the chord chart in the back of this book and get many chords as you need them. What is important is: What to do with chords once you have learned them. We need to learn methods of strumming and other variations that will make your folk accompaniments (and instrumental solos - eventually) more interesting.

The first step is to realize that your thumb may strike other strings in each chord beside the basic bass note. Your thumb may <u>alternate</u> from string to string as follows:

D Chord: Alternate between D string and A string.

A, A$_7$ and Am: Alternate between A string and E and/or D string.

G: Alternate between E string and A and/or D string.

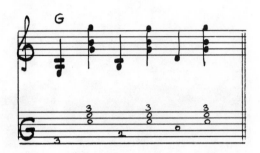

E$_7$ and Em: Alternate between E string and A string.

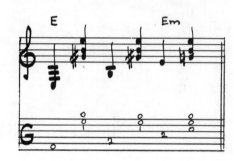

For all other chords the alternate bass strings will be indicated in the diagrams.

In $\frac{3}{4}$ time the alternation proceeds similarly. Just remember - two upstrokes for each downstroke.

KEY OF G MAJOR
IV and V$_7$ Chords

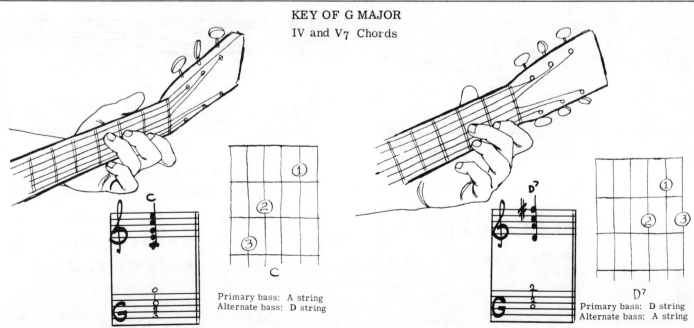

Primary bass: A string
Alternate bass: D string

Primary bass: D string
Alternate bass: A string

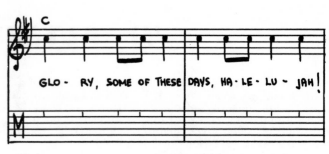

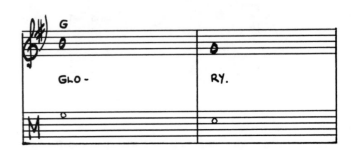

THE STREETS OF GLORY

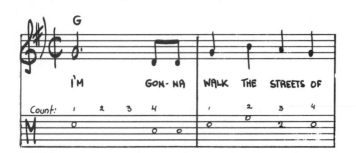

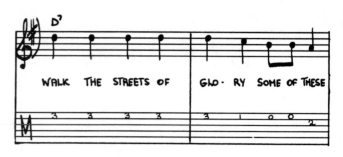

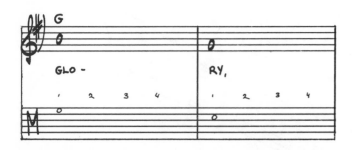

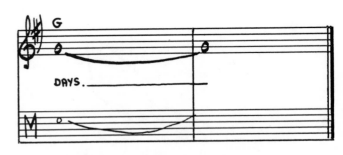

G
I'm gonna tell God how you treat me,
C
I'm gonna tell God how you treat me,

   One of these days, hallelujah.
G
I'm gonna tell God how you treat me,
D7
Tell God how you treat me one of these
   G
   days.

I'm gonna walk and talk with Jesus. . .

I WAS BORN ABOUT TEN THOUSAND YEARS AGO

G   D7
I saw Satan when he looked the Garden o'er,
                                               G
I saw Eve and Adam driven from the door,
     C   G
From behind the bushes peeping seen the apple they was

  eating
     D7   G
And I'll swear that I'm the guy what ate the core.

I taught Samson how to use his mighty hands,
Showed Columbus -- this happy land,
And for Pharoah's little kiddies built all the
    pyramiddies,
And to the Sahara carried all the sand.

I taught Solomon his little ABC's,
I was the first one ate Limburger cheese,
And while sailing down the bay with Methuselah one day,
I saved his flowing whiskers from the breeze.

Queen Elizabeth fell dead in love with me,
We were married in Milwaukee secretly,
But I snuck around and shook her, to go with General
    Hooker
To fight mosquiters down in Tennessee.

        Repeat the first verse

DANVILLE GIRL

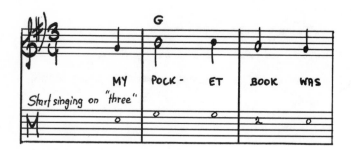

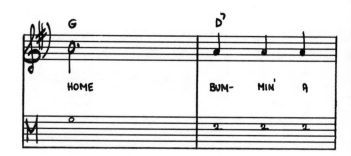

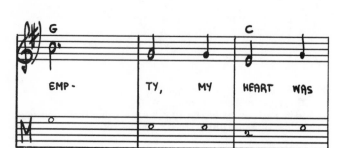

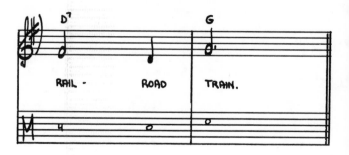

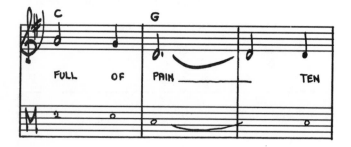

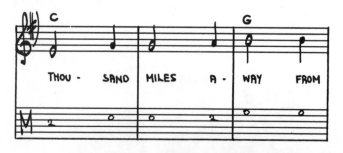

G   C   G
I was standing on the platform, smoking a cheap cigar,
G   D7   G
Waiting for the next freight train to carry an empty car.

When I got off at Danville, got stuck on a Danville girl,
You can bet your life she was out of sight, she wore
  those Danville curls.

She took me to her kitchen, she treated me nice
  an fine,
She got me out of the notion of bumming all the time.

She wore her hat on the back of her head, like
  high-tone people do,
But the very next train come down the line, I bid
  that girl adieu.

I pulled my cap down over my eyes, walked down to the
  railroad tracks;
There I caught the next freight train, never to
  come back.

KEY OF E MAJOR
I and V₇ Chords

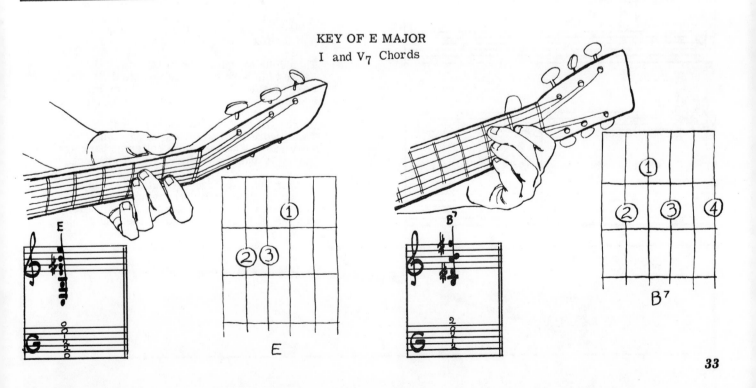

E

B⁷

THE FOX

The fox went out on a chil-ly night,

Prayed to the moon for to give him light for he'd

Man-y a mile to go that night be-

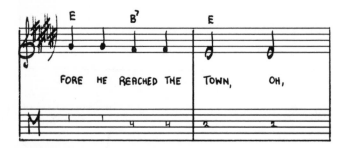

Fore he reached the town, oh,

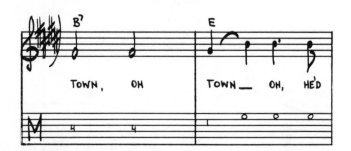

Town, oh Town___ oh, he'd

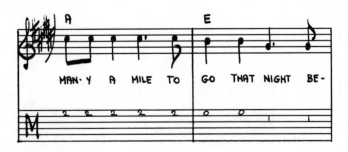

Man-y a mile to go that night be-

Fore he reached the town, oh.

E
He ran till he came to a great big pen,
                                    B7
Where the ducks and the geese were kept therein,
  E   A
A couple of you will grease my chin
  E   B7   E   B7   E
Before I leave this town, oh - town, oh - town, oh
  A   E
A couple of you will grease my chin
  B7   E
Before I leave this town, oh.

He grabbed the gray goose by the neck,
Throwed a duck across his back.
He didn't mind the quack, quack, quack,
And the legs all dangling down, oh...

The old Mrs. Flipper-Flopper jumped out of bed,
Out of the window she cocked her head,
Saying, "John, John, the goose is gone,
And the fox is on the town, oh..."

Then John he ran to top of the hill,
Blowed his horn both loud and shrill,
Fox, he said, "I better flee with my kill,
For they'll soon be on my trail, oh..."

He ran till he came to his cozy den,
There were the little ones: eight, nine, ten.
They said, "Daddy, you'd better go back again,
'Cause it must be a mighty fine town, oh..."

The fox and his wife, without any strife,
Cut up the goose with a carving knife.
They never had such a supper in their life,
And the little ones chewed on the bones, oh...

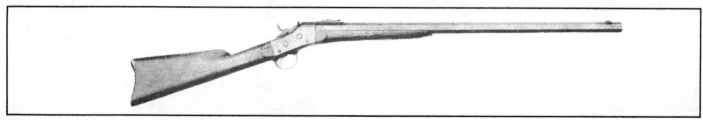

I RIDE AN OLD PAINT

Start singing on "three"

I RIDE AN OLD PAINT,— I

LEAD AN OLD DAN __ I'M GOIN' TO MON-

TA - NA TO THROW THE HOU - LI -

HAN, THEY FEED IN THE COU - LEES, THEY

WA - TER IN THE DRAW, THEIR TAILS ARE ALL

MAT - TED, THEIR BACKS ARE ALL RAW. RIDE A-

Chorus

ROUND, LIT - TLE DO - GIES, RIDE A-

ROUND THEM __ SLOW, FOR THE FIER - Y AND

SNUF - FY ARE RAR - IN' TO GO.

E
Old Bill Jones had two daughters and a song,
B7   E
One went to college the other went wrong.
   B7   E
His wife got killed in a pool-room fight,
   B7   E
But still he keeps singing from morning till night.

Chorus

I've worked in the city, worked on the farm,
And all I've got to show is the muscle in my arm.
Patches on my pants, callous on my hand
And I'm goin' to Montana to throw the houlihan.

Chorus

When I die, don't bury me at all,
Put me on my pony and lead him from his stall.
Tie my bone to his back, turn our faces to the west,
And we'll ride the prairie that we love the best.

Chorus

NEW YORK TOWN

Words and Music by Woody Guthrie
© Guthrie Childrens Trust Fund

STAND-ING DOWN IN NEW YORK TOWN ONE

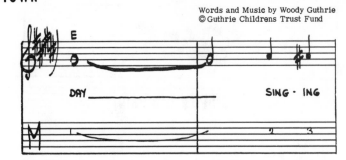

DAY ____ SING-ING

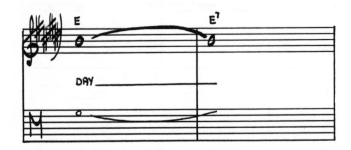

DAY ____

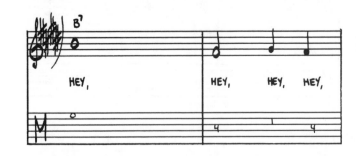

HEY, HEY, HEY, HEY,

STAND-ING DOWN IN NEW YORK TOWN ONE

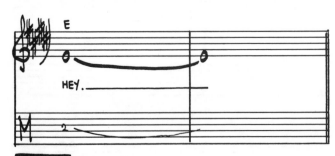

HEY.

CHORUS

DAY ____

HEY, HEY, HEY, HEY,

STAND-ING DOWN IN NEW YORK TOWN ONE

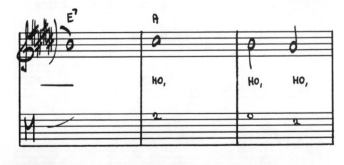

____ HO, HO, HO,

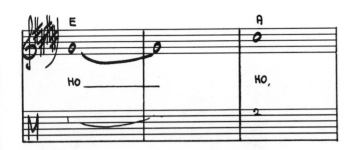

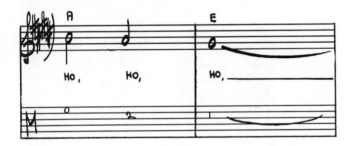

E   E-E7
I was broke, I did not have a dime,
A   E-E7
I was broke, I did not have a dime,
A   E
I was broke, I did not have a dime,
        B7   E
Singing, hey, hey, hey, hey.

Chorus

Every good man gets a little hard luck some time...

Chorus

I'm gonna catch that new morning train...

Chorus

Never coming back to this man's town again...

Chorus

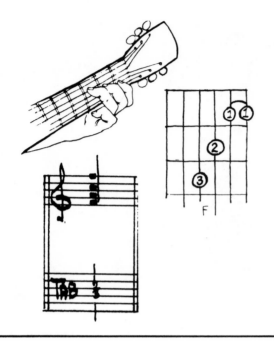

F

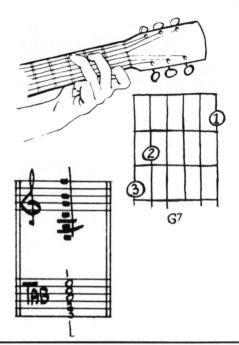

G7

BILLY BARLOW

LET'S GO HUNT-ING, SAYS RISK- Y

HUNT- ING SAYS DON- 'L TO JOE,

ROB, LET'S GO HUNT- ING, SAYS

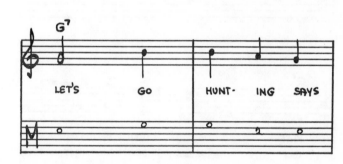

LET'S GO HUNT- ING SAYS

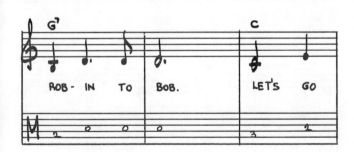

ROB- IN TO BOB. LET'S GO

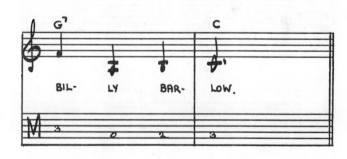

BIL- LY BAR- LOW.

     C
What shall I hunt? says Risky Rob,
                 G7
What shall I hunt? says Robin to Bob,
    C   F
What shall I hunt? says Dan'l to Joe,
  G7   C
Hunt for a rat, says Billy Barlow.

How shall I get him? says Risky Rob...
Go borrow a gun, says Billy Barlow.

How shall I haul him?...
Go borrow a wagon, says Billy Barlow.

How shall we divide him?...
How shall we divide him? says
    Billy Barlow.

I'll take shoulder, says Risky Rob,
I'll take side, says Robin to Bob,
I'll take ham, says Dan'l to Joe,
Tail bone mine, says Billy Barlow.

How shall we cook him?...
How shall we cook him? says
    Billy Barlow.

I'll broil shoulder, says Risky Rob,
I'll fry side, says Robin to Bob,
I'll boil ham, says Dan'l to Joe,
Tail bone raw, says Billy Barlow.

OH, SUSANNA

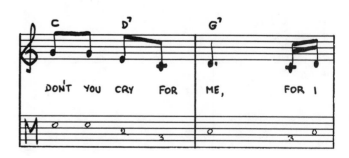

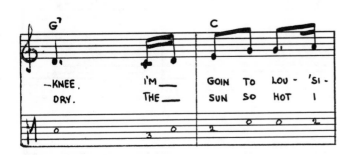

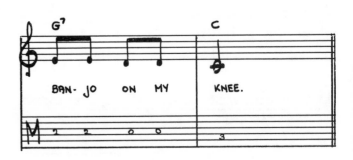

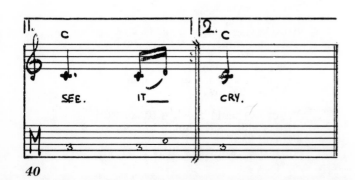

C
I had dream the other night
    D7   G7
When everything was still.
    C
I thought I saw Susanna
   G7   C
A-coming down the hill.

The buckwheat cake was in her mouth,
The tear was in her eye,
Says I, "I'm coming from the South,
Susanna, don't you cry."

Chorus

40

BUFFALO GALS

Chorus

C
Oh, yes pretty boys, we're coming out tonight,
G7   C
Coming out tonight, coming out tonight.

Oh, yes pretty boys, we're coming out tonight,
   G7   C
And dance by the light of the moon.

Chorus

I danced with a gal with a hole in her stockin',
And her heel kept a-rockin' and her toe kept a-knockin'
I danced with a gal with a hole in her stockin',
And we danced by the light of the moon.

Chorus

41

VII. A FAST "BANJO" STRUM

Finger an E chord.

1. Strike the bass note (E)
2. Brush lightly downward with fingernails over the rest of the strings.
3. Brush lightly upward with the first finger over the first couple of strings.
   (It doesn't matter here how many you strike.)

The rhythm looks like this:

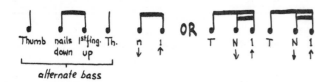

If you're not sure how this rhythmic pattern sounds, try saying

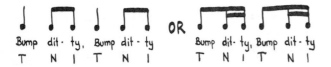

This is the way a 5-string banjo often sounds - though not played quite this way.

E-RI-E CANAL

HAD ONE NIGHT ON THE E- RI- E CA-

CHORUS

NAL. OH, THE E- RI- E WAS A-

RIS- ING, AND THE GIN WAS A GET- TING

LOW, AND I SCARCE-LY THINK WE'LL

GET A DRINK TILL WE GET TO BUF-FA-

LO,_____ TILL WE GET TO BUF-FA- LO.

E
We we're loaded down with barley,
                    B7   E
We we're chock full up on rye,
                 B7   E   A
And the captain he looked down at me
              E   B7   E
With his God damn' wicked eye.

Chorus

The captain he came up on deck
With a spyglass in his hand.
And the fog it was so gosh darn thick,
That he could not spy the land.

Chorus

Two days out of Syracuse
Our vessel struck a shoal,
And we like to all been drownded
On a chunk o' Lackawanna coal.

Chorus

Our cook she was a grand old gal,
She wore a ragged dress.
We hoisted her upon a pole
As a signal of distress.

Chorus

The captain, he got married,
And the cook, she went to jail.
And I'm the only son of a gun
That's left to tell the tale.

Chorus

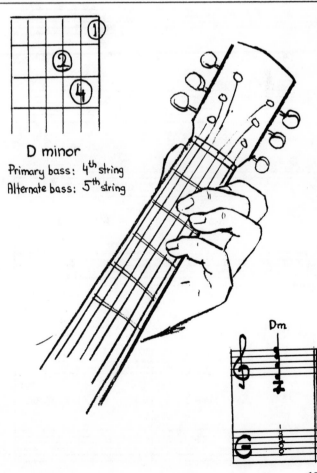

D minor
Primary bass: 4th string
Alternate bass: 5th string

Dm

43

LONESOME TRAVELLER

Words and Music by Lee Hayes and Walter Lowenfels
© Folkways Music Publishers

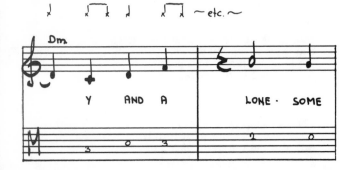

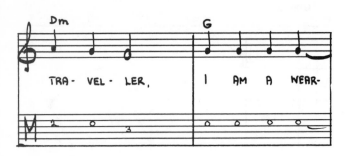

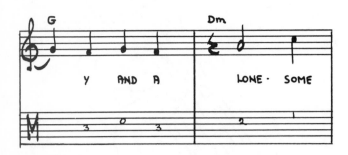

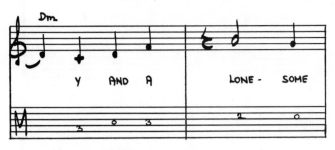

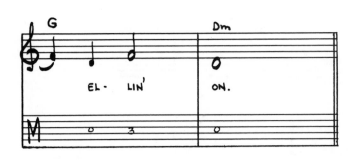

Dm
I've travelled cold and then I've

    travelled hungry, Lord.
G
I've travelled cold and then I've
  Dm
  travelled hungry, Lord.

I've travelled cold and then I've travelled

    hungry, Lord.
G
I've been a-travelling on.

Travelled with the rich, travelled with
    the poor...

Travelled in the mountains, travelled
    down in the valley...

One of these days I'm gonna stop
    all my travellin'...

Gonna keep right on a-travellin'
    on the road to freedom...

VIVA LA QUINCE BRIGADA

Am
En el frente de Jarama,
E
Rumbala, rumbala, rumbala. (2)
Am   G
No tenemos ni aviones,
                    F
Ni tanques, ni canones,
        E
Ay Manuela. (2)

Luchamos contra los morros...(2)
Mercenarios y fascistas...(2)

Solo es nuestro deseo...(2)
Acabar con el fascismo...(2)

Ya salimos de Espana...(2)
Por luchar en otras frentes...(2)

VIII. BASS RUNS

An endless series of "oom-pahs" - bass-chord, bass-chord, bass-chord... can soon get monotonous. In an effort to introduce more variety into your playing we now turn to a consideration of "bass runs". A bass run as the name implies, is a series of single notes played on the bass strings. These runs are usually played as a substitute for the last two or three beats of a chord just prior to the arrival of a new chord. In some cases they may themselves sound like a melody.

The actual series of notes which comprises a bass run is generally made up of the notes of the scale connecting the roots of the two chords involved. The following examples will illustrate:

Bass Runs in the Key of C

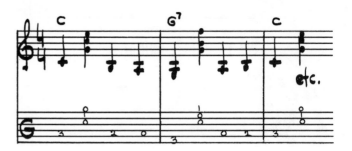

COTTON MILL GIRLS

C   F
I worked in the cotton mill all of my life
    C   G7
And I ain't got nothin' but a Barlow knife.
    C   F
It's hard times, cotton mill girls,
    C   G7   C
It's hard times everywhere.

Chorus

In 1915 we heard it said,
Move to the country and get ahead.
It's hard times...

Chorus

Us kids worked twelve hours a day
For fourteen cents of measly pay...

Chorus

When I die don't bury me at all,
Just hang me up on the spinning room wall.
Pickle my bones in alcohol,
It's hard times everywhere.

Chorus

MAKE ME A BED ON THE FLOOR

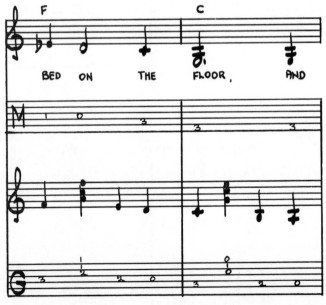

I'LL LAY MY HEAD ON THE

strum ~

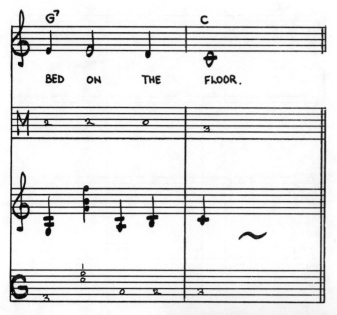

BED ON THE FLOOR.

C
Make me a bed right down on the floor, baby,
F   C
Make me a bed right down on the floor;
    G₇   C
And I'll lay my head on the bed on the floor.

Chorus

Clock striking midnight, daylight to go...

Chorus

Sheriff on my trail with a big forty-four...

Chorus

Bass Runs in Three-Quarter Time

ABDULLAH BULBUL AMIR

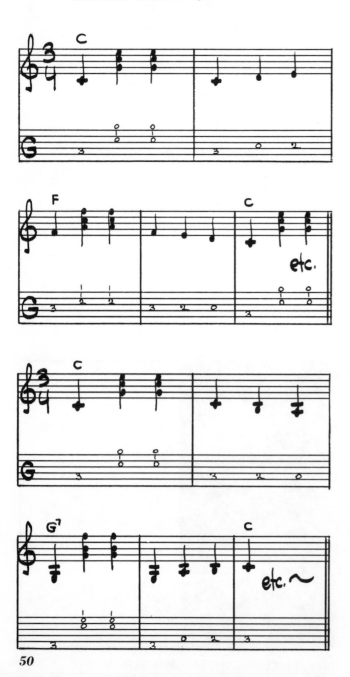

THE RANKS OF THE

PRO - PHET ARE HARD- Y AND BOLD, AND

50

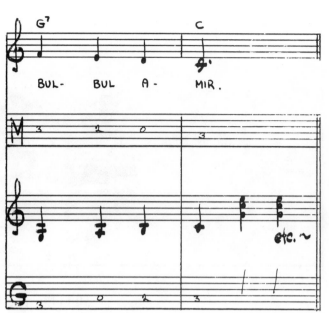

C   G7   C
When they needed a man to encourage the van,
   F   C
Or to harass a foe from the rear,
    G7   C
Storm fort or redoubt, they had only to shout
    G7   C
For Abdullah Bulbul Amir.

Now the heroes were plenty and well known to fame
Who fought in the ranks of the Czar;
But the bravest of these was a man by the name
Of Ivan Skavinsky Skivar.

He could imitate Irving, play poker and pool,
And strum on the Spanish guitar;
In fact, quite the cream of the Muscovite team
Was Ivan Skavinsky Skivar.

One day this bold Russian had shouldered his gun,
And donned his most truculent sneer;
Downtown he did go, where he trod on the toe
Of Abdullah Bulbul Amir.

"Young man", quoth Bulbul, "has your life grown so dull
That you're anxious to end your career?
Vile infidel, know, you have trod on the toe
Of Abdullah Bulbul Amir."

Said Ivan, "My friend, your remarks in the end
Will avail you but little, I fear;
For you ne'er will survive to repeat them alive,
Mr. Abdullah Bulbul Amir."

They fought all that night, 'neath the pale yellow moon,
The din, it was heard from afar,
And huge multitudes came, so great was the fame
Of Abdul and Ivan Skivar.

As Abdul's long knife was extracting the life,
In fact he had shouted, "Huzzah",
He felt himself struck by that wily Calmuck,
Count Ivan Skavinsky Skivar.

There's a tomb rises up where the Blue Danube rolls,
And 'graved there in characters clear
Are, "Stranger, when passing, oh, pray for the soul
Of Abdullah Bulbul Amir.

A Muscovite maiden, her lone vigil keeps
"Neath the light of the pale polar star,
And the name that she murmurs oft' as she weeps,
Is Ivan Skavinsky Skivar.

SO LONG, IT'S BEEN GOOD TO KNOW YOU

Words by (and music adapted by) Woody Guthrie
© Folkways Music Publishers

DUST IS A- GET- TING MY HOME _____

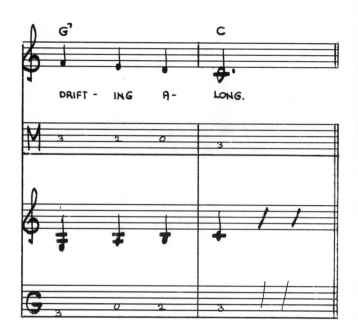

DRIFT - ING A- LONG.

_____ AND I'VE GOT TO BE

C   G7
The dust storm came and it hit us like thunder,
    C   G7
It dusted us over and covered us under,
    C   F
It blocked out the traffic, it blacked out the sun,
    C   G7   C
And straight for home all the people did run - singing

The sweethearts sat in the dark and they sparked.
They hugged and they kissed in that dusty old dark,
The sighed and they cried and they hugged and they kissed,
Instead of marriage they talked like this: Honey

The telephone rang and it jumped off the wall,
And it was they preacher a-making a call.
He said, "Kind friend, this may be the end,
You've got your last chance at salvation of sin". Well, it's

The churches was jammed and the churches was packed.
That dusty old dust storm blowed so darn black
That the preacher could not read a word of his text,
So he took up collection and folded his specks, singing

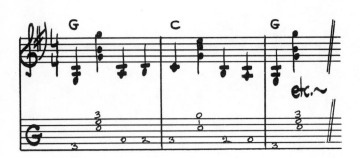
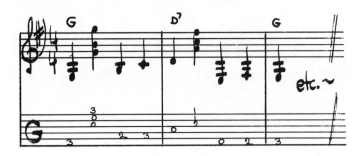

SHE'LL BE COMIN' 'ROUND THE MOUNTAIN

SHE'LL BE COM-IN' 'ROUND THE MOUN-TAIN WHEN SHE

strum ~

COMES, SHE'LL BE COM-IN' 'ROUND THE MOUN-TAIN WHEN SHE

COMES,   SHE'LL BE

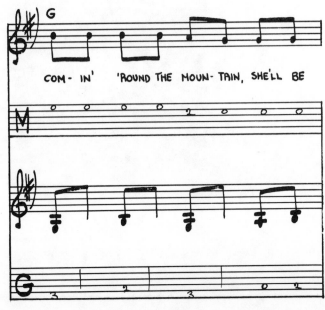

COM-IN'   'ROUND THE MOUN-TAIN, SHE'LL BE

COM - IN' 'ROUND THE MOUN - TAIN, SHE'LL BE

COM - IN' 'ROUND THE MOUN - TAIN WHEN SHE COMES.

G
She'll be riding six white horses when she comes,
                                          D7
She'll be riding six white horses when she comes,
 G   C
She'll be riding six white horses, she'll be riding six

   white horses,
      D7   G
She'll be riding six white horses when she comes.

Oh, we'll all go out to meet her when she comes (2)
Oh, we'll all go out to meet her and we'll all be glad
     to greet her,
Oh, we'll all go out to meet her when she comes.

Oh, we'll kill the old red rooster... 'cause he don't
    crow like he used ter...

CAN'T YOU DANCE THE POLKA?

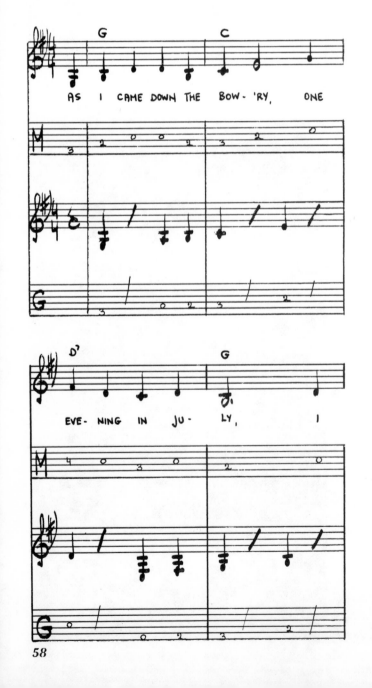

AS I CAME DOWN THE BOW - 'RY, ONE

EVE - NING IN JU - LY, I

MET A MAID WHO ASKED MY TRADE, AND A

SAIL - OR JOHN, SAID I ____ THEN A -

WAY, YOU SAN-TY,

MY DEAR AN-NIE,

OH, YOU NEW YORK GIRLS,

CAN'T YOU DANCE THE POL-KA.

Says she, "You lime-juice sailor, now see me home
    you may."
But when we reached her cottage door she unto me
    did say.

Chorus

"My young man he's a sailor, with his hair cut short behind;
He wears a tarry jumper, and he saile the Black Ball Line."

Chorus

G   C   D₇   G
To Tiffany's I took her, I did not mind expense,
                  C
I bought her two gold earrings
                   D₇   G
           - they cost me fifty cents.

Chorus

59

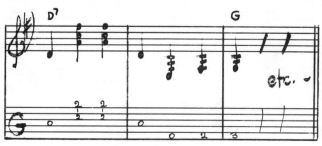

SANTA LUCIA

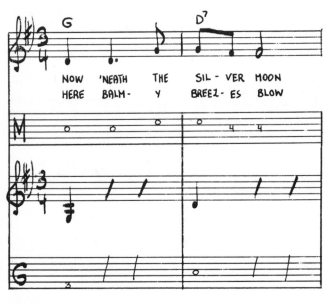

NOW 'NEATH THE SIL-VER MOON
HERE BALM-Y BREEZ-ES BLOW

BIL-LOWS SOFT WINDS ARE BLOW-ING
GENT-LY ROW, ALL THINGS DE-LIGHT US

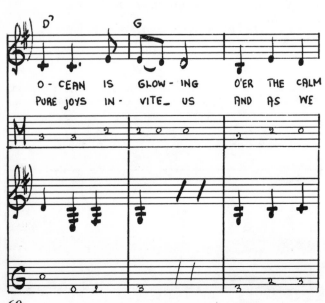

O-CEAN IS GLOW-ING O'ER THE CALM
PURE JOYS IN-VITE_ US AND AS WE

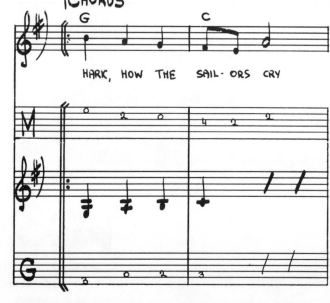

CHORUS

HARK, HOW THE SAIL-ORS CRY

G   D7   G
When o'er the waters light winds are playing,
                D7   G
Thy spell can sooth us, all care allaying.
G   D7   G
To thee, sweet Napoli, what charms are given,
                D7   G
Where smiles creation, toil blessed by Heaven.

Chorus

BENDEMEER'S STREAM

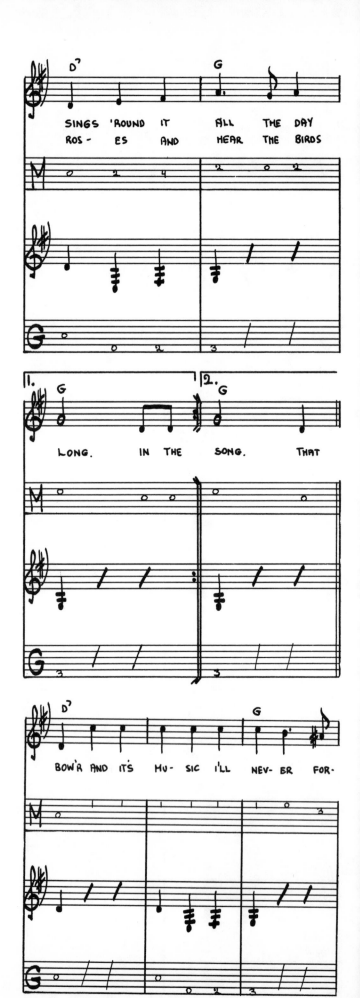

GET, BUT OFT WHEN A-LONE IN THE

BLOOM OF THE YEAR I THINK; "IS THE

NIGHT-IN-GALE SING-ING THERE YET? ARE THE

ROS-ES STILL BRIGHT BY THE

CALM BEN-DE-MEER?"

RED RIVER VALLEY

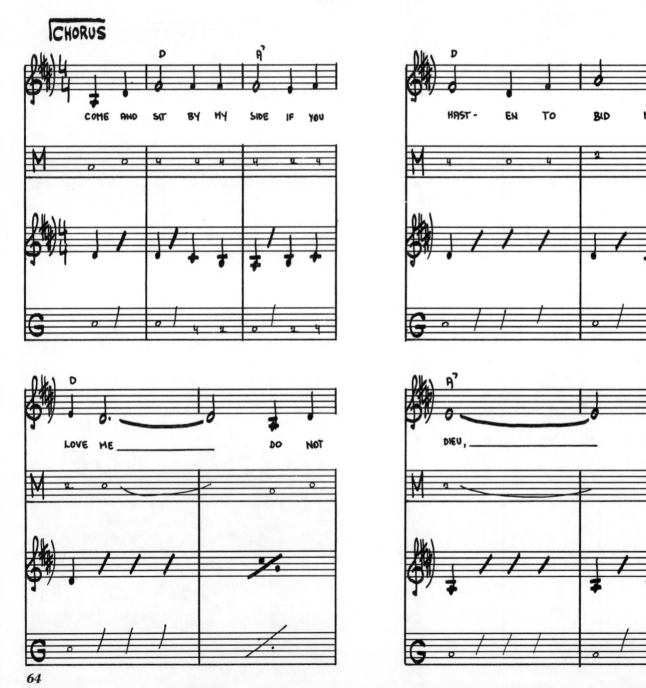

COME AND SIT BY MY SIDE IF YOU HAST-EN TO BID ME A-

LOVE ME _____ DO NOT DIEU, _____ BUT RE-

MEM- BER THE RED RIV- ER

TRUE. _____

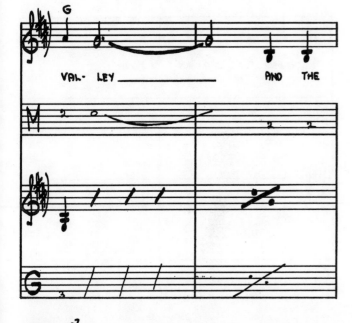

VAL- LEY _____ AND THE

D   A7   D
Won't you think of this valley you're leaving,
                              A7
Oh, how lonely, how sad it will be,
          D
Oh, think of the fond heart you're breaking,
     A7   D
And the grief you are causing me.

Chorus

From this valley they say you are going,
When you go may your darling go, too?
Would you leave her behind unprotected
When she loves no other but you?

Chorus

GIRL THAT HAS LOVED YOU SO

MY HOME'S ACROSS THE SMOKY MOUNTAINS

CROSS THE SMO - KY MOUN -

MORE AND I'LL NE - VER GET TO

TAINS, AND I'LL NE - VER GET TO

SEE YOU AN - Y - MORE.

SEE YOU AN - Y - MORE, MORE,

D
Goodbye, honey, sugar darling,
A7
Goodbye, honey, sugar darling,   D

Goodbye, honey, sugar darling,
        A7   D
And I'll never get to see you any more, more, more,
    G   A7   D
I'll never get to see you any more.

Rock my honey feed her candy...(3)
And I'll never...

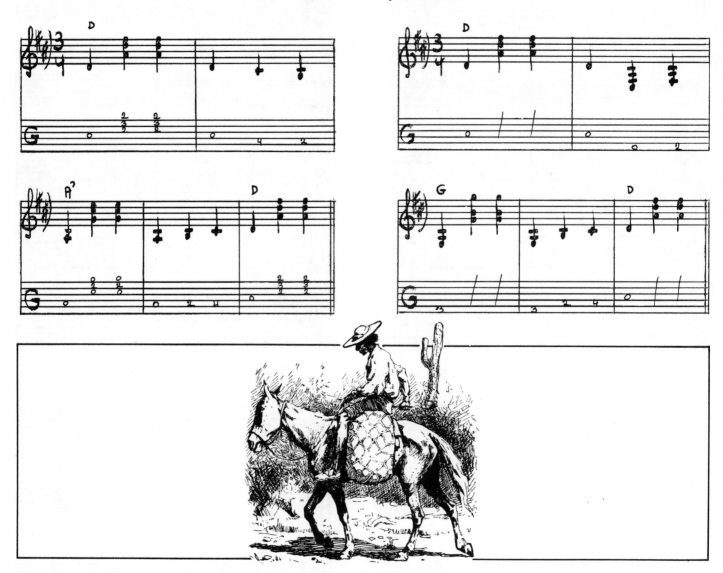

LITTLE MOHEE

AS I WENT OUT WALK-ING

UP - ON A FINE

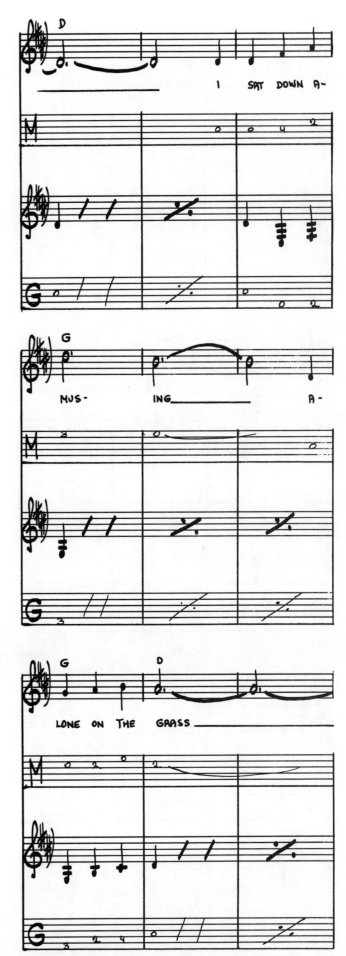

WHEN WHO SHOULD SIT BY ME

LASS.

BUT A SWEET IN- DIAN

D   A7   D
She sat down beside me upon a fine day,
        A7   D
I got awful lonesome as the day passed away.
              G   D
She asked me to marry, and gave me her hand,
              A7   D
Said, "My pappy's a chieftain all over this land."

"My pappy's a chieftain and ruler be he,
I'm his only daughter and my name is Mohee."
I answered and told her that it never could be,
'Cause I had my own sweetheart in my own country.

I had my own sweetheart and I knew she loved me.
Her heart was as true as any Mohee.
So I said, "I must leave you and goodbye my dear,
There's a wind in my canvas and home I must steer."

At home with relations I tried for to see,
But there wasn't one there like my little Mohee;
And the girl I had trusted proved untrue to me,
So I sailed o'er the ocean to my little Mohee.

THE FOUR MARYS

LAST NIGHT THERE WERE__ FOUR

strum___

MA- RYS, TO- NIGHT THERE'LL

BE__ BUT THREE. _____ THERE WAS

MI - CHLE AND ME.

MA - RY SEA- TON AND MA - RY

BEA- TON AND MA - RY CAR -

D   G   D
Oh, often have I dressed my queen

And put on her braw silk gown,
     D   G   D   G
But all the thanks I've got tonight,
    Em   A7   D
Is to be hanged in Edinborough Town.

Full often have I dressed my queen,
Put gold upon her hair,
But I have got for my reward
The gallows to be my share.

Oh, little did my mother know,
The day she cradled me,
The land I was to travel in,
The death I was to dee.

Oh, happy, happy is the maid
That's born of beauty free;
Oh, it was my rosy dimpled cheeks
That's been the devil to me.

They'll tie a kerchief around my eyes,
That I may not see to dee,
And they'll never tell my father or mother
But that I'm across the sea.

repeat verse one

Here is a more common fingering for E₇

E⁷

Primary bass: E string
Alternate bass: A & D string

FRANKIE AND JOHNNY

~ strum ~

FRAN- KIE AND JOHN- NY WERE

LOV- ERS OH, LORD- Y HOW_ THEY COULD

LOVE. SWORE TO BE TRUE_ TO EACH

A
Frankie and Johnny went walking,

Johnny in his brand-new suit.
D
"Oh, Good Lord", said Frankie,
                                        A
"Don't my Johnny man look cute?"
E7   A
He was her man, but he done her wrong.

Johnny said, "I've got to leave you,
"But I won't be very long.
"Don't wait up for me, honey,
"Or worry while I'm gone,"
He was her man...

Frankie went down to the corner,
Went in the saloon for some beer.
She said to the fat bartender,
"Has my Johnny man been here?"
He was her man...

"Well, I ain't gonna tell you no story,
"And I ain't gonna tell you no lie.
"I saw your Johnny 'bout an hour ago
"With a gal named Nellie Bly.
"If he's your man, he's a-doin you wrong".

Frankie got off at South 12th Street,
She didn't go there for fun,
For under her long red kimono
She carried a forty-four gun.
He was her man...

Frankie went into the hotel,
Looked up in the window so high.
There she saw her Johnny
A-lovin' up Nellie Bly.
He was her man...

Johnny saw Frankie a-comin',
Down the backstairs he did scoot.
Frankie pulled out her pistol
And the gun went rooty-toot-toot.
He was her man, but she shot him down.

"Roll me over so easy,
"Roll me over so slow.
"Roll me over on my right side,
"For my left side hurts me so.
"I was her man, but I done her wrong."

Bring out your rubber-tired hearses,
Bring out your old-time hack.
Twelve men going to the graveyard
And eleven coming back.
He was her man...

"Oh, bring out a thousand policemen,
"Lock me into your cell,
"For I've shot my Johnny so dead
"I know I'm going to hell.
"He was my man, but I shot him down."

Frankie mounted to the scaffold
As calm as a girl could be,
And turning her eyes to heaven
She said, "Nearer, my God, to Thee".
He was her man...

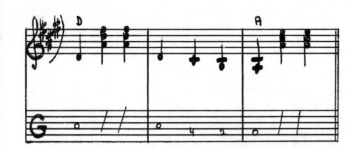

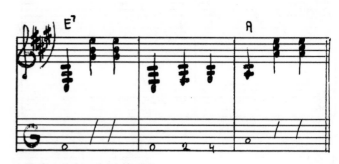

SWEET BETSY FROM PIKE

OH, DON'T YOU RE- MEM- BER SWEET

BET- SY FROM PIKE, WHO CROSSED THE BIG

75

A   E7   A
One evening quite early they camped on the Platte,
          B7   E7
'Twas near by the road on a green shady flat;
     A   D   A
Where Betsy, quite tired lay down to repose,
          E7   A
While with wonder Ike gazed on his Pike County rose.

Chorus

They swam the wide rivers and crossed the tall peaks,
And camped on the prairie for weeks upon weeks,
Starvation and cholera, hard work and slaughter,
They reached California spite of hell and high water.

Chorus

Out on the prairie one bright starry night
They broke out the whisky and Betsy got tight.
She sang and she shouted and danced o'er the plain,
And showed her bare arse to the whole wagon train.

Chorus

They reached the hot desert where Betsy gave out,
And down in the sand she lay rolling about,
While Ike in great wonder looked on in surprise,
Saying, "Betsy, get up, you'll get sand in your eyes."

Chorus

Long Ike and Sweet Betsy were married, of course.
But Ike, growing jealous, obtained a divorce,
And Betsy, well satisfied, said with a shout,
"Goodbye, you big lummox, I'm glad you backed out!"

Chorus

Bass Runs in the Key of E

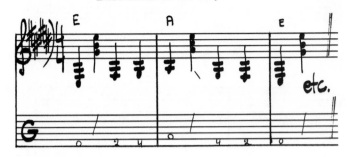

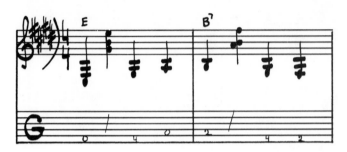

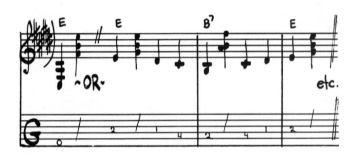

CARELESS LOVE

LOVE,   OH   LOVE,   OH   CARE-LESS

E   B7   E
I cried last night and the night before,
              B7
I cried last night and the night before,
E   A
I cried last night and the night before,
  E B7   E
Gonna cry tonight and cry no more

I love my momma and my poppa too (3x)
But I'd leave them both to go with you.

When I wore my apron low (3x)
You'd follow me through rain and snow.

Now I wear my apron high (3x)
You see my door and pass right by.

Love, oh, love...

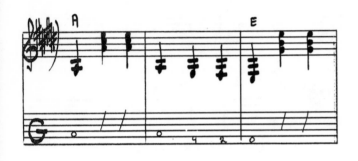

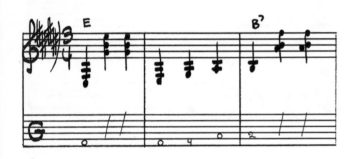

GREEN GROW THE LILACS

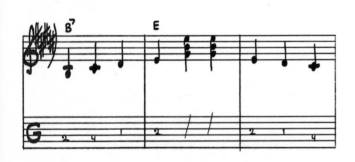

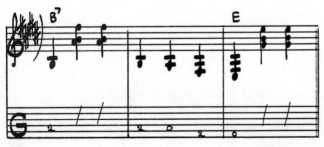

Strum

GREEN GROW THE LI- LACS ALL

SPARK- LING WITH DEW, I'M

LONE-LY MY DAR-LING SINCE PART-ING WITH

strum~

LI-LACS TO THE RED, WHITE AND BLUE.

YOU, BUT BY OUR NEXT MEET-ING I

E
I used to have a sweetheart, but now I

have none,

                         B7
Since she's gone and left me, I care

not for one.

          E   A
Since she's gone and left me, contented

I'll be,

E   B7
For she loves another one better

            E
than me.

HOPE TO PROVE TRUE, AND CHANGE THE GREEN

I passed my love's window, both early
   and late,
The look that she gave me, it made my
   heart ache.
Oh, the look that she gave me was
   painful to see,
For she loves another one better than
   me.

I wrote my love letters in rosy red
   lines,
She sent me an answer all twisted in
   twines,
Saying, "Keep your love letters and I
   will keep mine,
Just you write to your love and I'll
   write to mine."

Repeat Verse 1

IX. ARPEGGIOS

This is one of the many words in the lexicon of music which is borrowed from the Italian. It comes from the word arpa - harp. You all know how a harp sounds when its strings are plucked one at a time. Chords played in this manner are called "arpeggios". There are many different kinds of arpeggio patterns. Sometimes they give a very lyrical quality to songs such as Greensleeves or Shenandoah. Other times they may enhance the rhythmic feeling of John Henry or a blues.

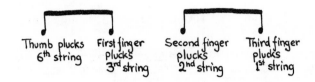

Thumb plucks 6th string — First finger plucks 3rd string — Second finger plucks 2nd string — Third finger plucks 1st string

IMPORTANT — The fingers of the right hand are placed on the proper strings all at the same time. Each finger remains in contact with its string until it has to pluck that string. Don't move your wrist while playing the arpeggio.

RIDDLE SONG

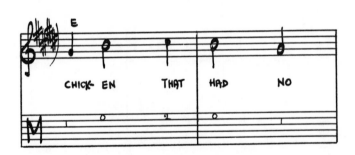

END, I GAVE MY LOVE A

BA - BY WITH NO CRY - IN'.

E   A   E
How can there be a cherry that has no stone,
 B7   E   B7
How can there be a chicken that has no bone,
      E   B7
How can there be a story that has no end,
 E   A   E
How can there be a baby with no cryin'.

A cherry, when it's blooming, it has no stone,
A chicken, when it's pipping, it has no bone,
The story that I love you, it has no end,
A baby, when it's sleeping has no cryin'.

THE CRUEL WAR

Guitar rhythm:

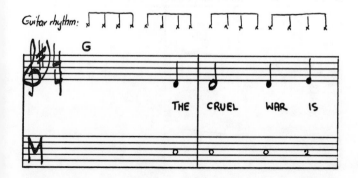

THE CRUEL WAR IS

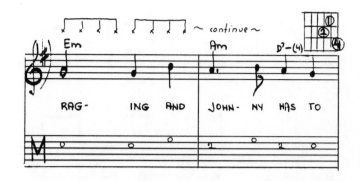

RAG - ING AND JOHN - NY HAS TO

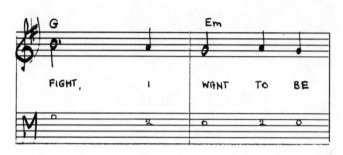

FIGHT, I WANT TO BE

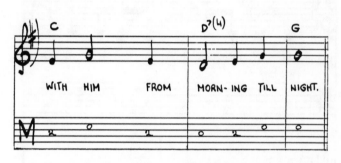

WITH HIM FROM MORN - ING TILL NIGHT.

G   Em   Am D7(4) G
I'll go to your captain, get down upon my knees,
   Em   C   D7(4)   G
Ten thousand gold guineas I'd give for your release.

Ten thousand gold guineas, it grieves my heart so;
Won't you let me go with you? - Oh, no, my love, no.

Tomorrow is Sunday and Monday is the day
Your captain calls for you, and you must obey.

Your captain calls for you, it grieves my heart so,
Won't you let me go with you? - Oh, no, my love, no.

Your waist is too slender, your fingers are too small,
Your cheeks are to rosy to face the cannonball.

Your cheeks are to rosy, it grieves my heart so,
Won't you let me go with you? Oh, no, my love, no.

Johnny, oh Johnny, I think you are unkind,
I love you far better than all other mankind.

I love you far better than tongue can express,
Won't you let me go with you? Oh, yes, my love, yes.

I'll pull back my hair, men's clothes I'll put on,
I'll pass for your comrade as we march along.

I'll pass for your comrade and none will ever guess,
Won't you let me go with you? - Yes, my love, yes.

You may alternate a "regular" bass-chord strum with an arpeggio. Make sure that faster "one-and two-and" of the arpeggio takes the same time to play as the "one-two" of the bass-chord strum. (Bass runs may be combined in the same song with arpeggios.)

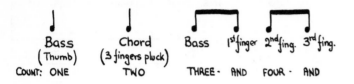

DRILL, YE TARRIERS, DRILL

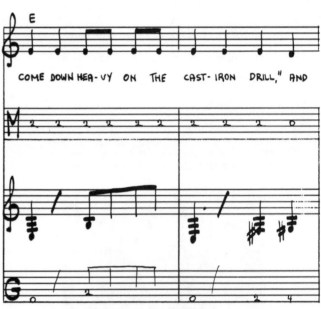

82

Am
Now, our new foreman was Jim McCann,
   E
By God, he was a blame mean man,
    Am
Last week a premature blast went off,
   E
And a mile in the air went Big Jim Goff,
   Am   E   Am
And drill, ye tarriers, drill.

Chorus

The next time payday come around,
Jim Goff a dollar short was found
When he asked, "What for?", came this reply,
"You're docked for the time you was up in the sky,"
And drill, ye tarriers, drill. (chorus)

Now, the boss was a fine man down to the ground,
And he married a lady six feet round;
She baked good bread and she baked it well,
But she baked it hard as the holes in hell,
And drill, ye tarriers, drill.

Chorus

KATIUSHA

APPLE TREES AND
RASTSVETALI

RIVER MIST WAS
POPLYLI TU-

PEAR TREES WERE A-FLOWER,
YA-BLONI I GRU-SHI,

RISING ALL A-ROUND.
MANI NAD REKOI.

YOUNG KA - TIU - SHA WENT
VY - KHO - DI - LA

O'ER THE ROCK - Y GROUND.
BE - REG, NA KRU - TOI.

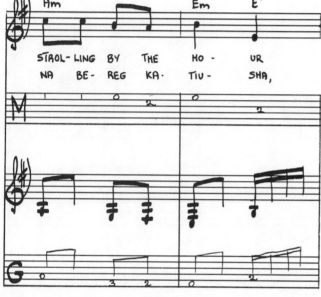

STROL - LING BY THE HO - UR
NA BE - REG KA - TIU - SHA,

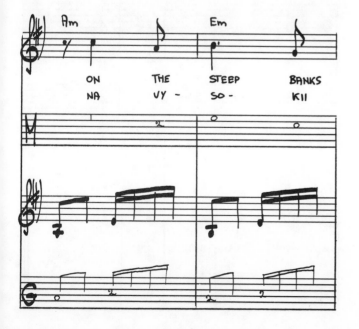

ON THE STEEP BANKS
NA VY - SO - KII

Em   B7
By the river's bank she sang a love song
                             Em
Of her hero in a distant land.
Em C G E7   Am   Em E7
Of the one she'd dearly loved for so long,
Am   Em   B7   Em
Holding tight his letters in her hand.   (2)

Oh, you song, song of a maiden's true love,
To my dear one travel with the sun.
To the one with whom Katiusha knew love,   (2)
Bring my greetings to him one by one.

Let him know that I am true and faithful,
Let him hear the love song that I send,
Tell him as he defends our home that grateful (2)
True Katiusha our love will defend.

Repeat verse one

Vykhodila, pesniu zavodila
Pro stepnovo sizovo orla,
Pro tovo, kotorovo liubila,   (2)
Pro tovo, chi pisma beregla.

Oi ty, pesnia, pesenka devichia,
Ty leti za yasnym sontsem vsled,
I boitsu na dalnem pograniche   (2)
Ot Katiushi peredai privet,

Pust on vspomnit devushku prostuyu,
Pust uslyshit, kak ana payot,
Pust on zemliu berezhot rodnuyu, (2)
A liubov Katiusha sberezhot.

Arpeggios in $\frac{3}{4}$ Time

Finger a D chord.

This arpeggio may be alternated with the basic "bass-chord-chord" of a "regular" $\frac{3}{4}$ strum. In this case the six beats of the arpeggio (one-and two-and three-and") take the same time as the original "oom-pah-pah" ("one-two-three").

POOR BOY

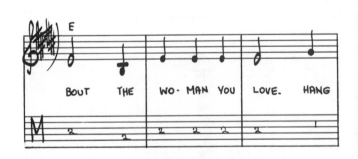

```
E        B7      E        E7
As I went down to the river, poor boy,
   A              E
To see the ships go by,

My sweetheart stood on the deck of one,
                        B7      E
And she waved to me goodbye.


Chorus (sung occasionally)


I followed her for months and months,
She offered me her hand.
We were just about to be married, when
She ran off with a gambling man

He came at me with a big jack-knife,
I went for him with lead,
And when the fight was over, poor boy,
He lay down beside me, dead.

They took me to the big jail-house,
The months and months rolled by.
The jury found me guilty, poor boy,
And the judge said, "You must die."

Oh do you bring me silver, poor boy,
Or do you bring me gold?
"I bring you neither", said the man,
"I bring you a hangman's fold."

Oh do you bring me pardon, poor boy,
To turn me a-loose?
"I bring you nothing said the man,
Except a hangman's noose."

And yet they call this justice, poor boy,
Then justice let it be!
I only killed a man that was
A fixin' to kill me.
```

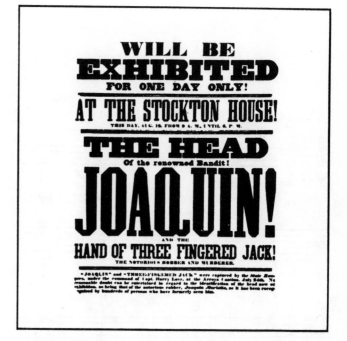

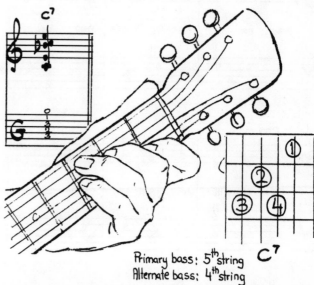

Primary bass: 5th string
Alternate bass: 4th string

C7

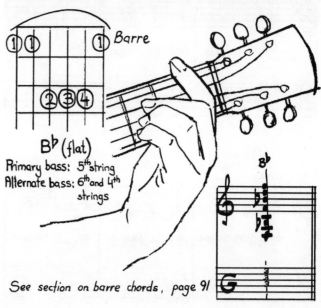

B♭ (flat)
Primary bass: 5th string
Alternate bass: 6th and 4th strings

See section on barre chords, page 91

HENRY MARTIN

Guitar rhythm:

THERE WERE THREE
BROTH-ERS IN MER-RY SCOT-LAND, IN

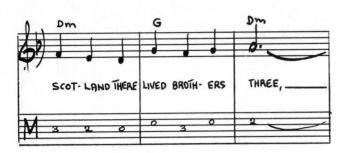

SCOT-LAND THERE LIVED BROTH-ERS THREE,

AND THEY DID CAST LOTS WHICH

OF THEM SHOULD GO SHOULD GO, SHOULD

GO, FOR TO TURN

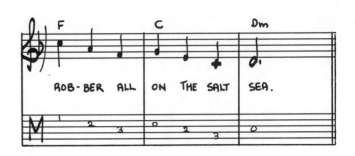

ROB-BER ALL ON THE SALT SEA.

Dm   C Dm
The lot it fell upon Henry Martin,
     G Dm - A7
The youngest of all the three,

That he should turn robber all on the salt sea,
   C7 F - A7
 salt sea, salt sea,
Bb(Dm) F   C   Dm
For to maintain his two brothers and he.

He had not been sailing but a long winter's night,
And part of a short winter's day,
When he espi-ed a lofty stout ship, stout ship, stout ship,
Come a-bibbing down on him straightway.

"Hello, hello", cried Henry Martin,
What makes you sail so high?
"I'm a rich merchant ship bound for fair London
  Town, London Town, London Town,
Will you please for to let me pass by?"

"Oh no, oh no," cried Henry Martin,
"That thing it never can be,
For I have turned robber all on the salt sea, salt
  sea, salt sea,
For to maintain my two brothers and me."

With broadside and broadside and at it they went
For fully two hours or three,
Till Henry Martin gave to her the death shot,
  the death shot, the death shot,
Heavily listing to starboard went she.

The rich merchant vessel was wounded full sore,
And straight to the bottom went she,
And Henry Martin sailed away on the sea,
  salt sea, salt sea,
For to maintain his two brothers and he.

Bad news, bad news to old England came,
Bad news to fair London Town,
There was a rich vessel and she's cast away,
And all of her merry men drowned.

X. TRANSPOSING

The process of changing a song from one key to another is known as transposing. For the folk guitarist an understanding of how to transpose is absolutely vital because any song in any given key may not be in his comfortable vocal range: it may either be too high or too low.

When we sing a song in the key of, say, A that means that A is the "starting point" and the "finishing point" of the song. The other chords in A somehow seem to revolve around A - always returning to it. What are those other chords? The most important other chords in A are (as you know) D and E_7. If we visualize the musical (alphabetical) scale we will soon see that if A is the first note of that scale then D is the fourth and E is the fifth.

$$1 \quad 2 \quad 3 \quad 4 \quad 5 \quad 6 \quad 7$$
$$(A, B, C^\#, D, E, F^\#, G^\#)$$

This I, IV, V relationship occurs in all major keys and is the very backbone of harmony as we know it in the western world.

In the five major keys we have learned so far the I (called "tonic"), IV ("sub-dominant") and V ("dominant") chords are

KEY	I	IV	V7
C	C	F	G_7
G	G	C	D_7
D	D	G	A_7
A	A	D	E_7
E	E	A	B_7

The chords of any key are completely interchangeable - that is, transposable - with the chords of any other key provided the correct numerical (I, IV, V) relationship is preserved.

The following example will illustrate.

YANKEE DOODLE

I	V7	I	V7
C	G7	C	G7
G	D7	G	D7
D	A7	D	A7
A	E7	A	E7
E	B7	E	B7

Yankee Doodle went to town, riding on his pony,

I	IV	V7	I
C	F	G7	C
G	C	D7	G
D	G	A7	D
A	D	E7	A
E	A	B7	E

Stuck a feather in his hat and called it macaroni.

If there are more than three chords in a song it is still possible to transpose it to another key. However, here a knowledge of key signatures (sharps and flats) is necessary. The following reference table will illustrate.

Key	Notes of the Scale						
	1	2	3	4	5	6	7
C	C	D	E	F	G	A	B
G	G	A	B	C	D	E	F#
D	D	E	F#	G	A	B	C#
A	A	B	C#	D	E	F#	G#
E	E	F#	G#	A	B	C#	D#

The relationships between the notes of the scales of all the major keys is gone into in greater detail in The Folksinger's Guitar Guide, Vol. 2.

XI. ODDS AND ENDS

TUNING THE GUITAR

The customary first step in the study of a stringed instrument is to teach the student how to tune it. While this may seem like the obvious beginning there are a number of difficulties to be overcome.

A sense of pitch - the ability to determine the relative "highness" and "lowness" - of notes, while indispensable to a musician, may not be present in its most sensitive, refined degree at the beginning of study.

The determination of whether one string is higher or lower than "it should be" is a highly sophisticated process. And even if that determination has been made, "what to do about it" may cause further problems.

When you start comparing notes on the guitar to supposedly corresponding notes on the piano or the pitch pipe you have to be able to discount the obvious (and sometimes confusing) difference in tonal quality - timbre - (a piano doesn't really sound like a guitar) - to distinguish tonal quality from pitch variation.

It is the rare, fortunate beginner who is able to "hear his way through" all this and come up with an in-tune instrument.

However, a sense of pitch can be developed, trained and refined in most people so that "after a while" (a necessarily vague expression) guitars do get tuned.

Therefore, the following information on tuning is presented here more for reference - present and future - than to be mastered before any further progress is made on the guitar.

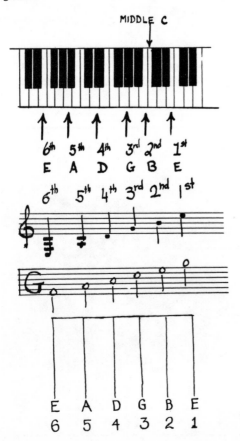

If the string you are tuning is too low in comparison with the piano you must tighten it to raise the pitch, if it is too high it must be loosened. As you turn the tuning gear remember to keep playing the string to hear which way it is going and to know when to stop.

Notice that the interval between the 6th and 5th strings (E f g A) is four notes. More precisely, it is called a "perfect fourth". A to D is also a perfect fourth - likewise D to G. The next pair of strings are a "major third" apart (G a B) and the last two (B-E) are a perfect fourth again.

A Pitchpipe - is a little whistle or set of whistles tuned to one - or all six - of the strings of the guitar. A common 6 note pitch pipe looks like this:

The one great advantage of a pitch pipe over a piano is that it fits into your guitar case easier than a piano.

The internal relationship between the strings - or "relative pitch" - leads us to another way of tuning commonly used when no standard pitch (like a piano or pitchpipe) is present.

1) Assume your lowest string is fairly on pitch.

2) Press that string down just below the 5th fret.

   The 5th string, next to it, should now sound the same pitch.

3) Now press the 5th string down at the 5th fret.

   The 4th string should now sound this pitch.

4) Press the 4th string down at the same place and the third string should sound the same pitch.

5) Press the third string down just below the 4th fret, and it should sound the same as the 2nd string.

6) Press the 2nd string down just below the 5th fret again, and tune the 1st string to it. The 1st string should now be just exactly two octaves above the 6th string.

As you become more experienced your initial assumption as to the correctness of the pitch of the 6th string will be less fanciful. A good guitar player may not have "perfect pitch" (a gift of the Gods) but he will be able to tell pretty accurately if his starting point is anywhere near the mark.

The final stage in tuning by relative pitch is achieved when one can play, say, the 6th string and <u>hear</u> "in advance" what the others should sound like.

That may take a while...

THE BARRE

The barre (pronounced "bar") is usually the index finger of the left hand which presses down tightly over all six strings at a particular fret and enables the remaining three fingers to play a chord. Barre chords are as necessary to a guitarist's technique as "non-barre" chords. Indeed, a chord is a chord is a chord - no matter where it may be found.

To play a barre properly it is necessary for the index finger to remain relatively rigid - at least, not to bend. Any undue curvature in the finger will mean that consistent pressure is not being maintained upon all the strings - and that ain't good!

One startling fact about a barre chord is that you get eleven for the price of one. If you learn, for example, these four patterns (two major, two minor - there are others) you will have added 44 new chords to your collection!

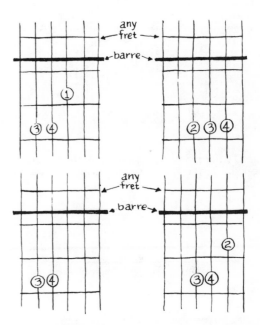

Check the chord page to find out what these chords are.

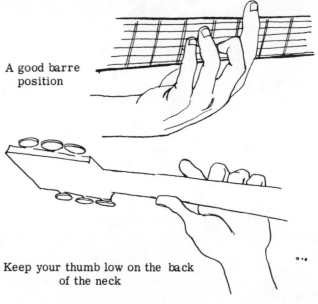

A good barre position

Keep your thumb low on the back of the neck

THE CAPO

Some day you may come across someone who sings Skip To My Lou in the key of E-flat (Yes, there is such a key). It's not entirely unrealistic to expect a guitarist to be able to execute this little musical nicety. Or, perhaps someone might want to sing Joshua Fought The Battle of Jericho in the key of C minor. Again, this, too, can be done by learning to play in C minor. On the other hand, playing comfortably in E flat or C minor might take several years of study and what do you do about those songs in the meantime?

What do you do...? You take your capo and you clamp it across the first fret of your guitar and you finger a D chord (counting up the proper number of frets from the capo) and voila! E flat.

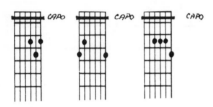

For C minor and its associated chords you would put the capo at the third fret and finger in the key of A minor.

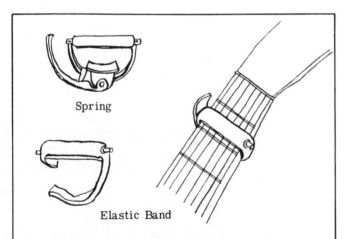

Note: There are many different makes of capos on the market ranging in price from 50¢ to several dollars, and involving different types of springs, bands, and bars.

How would you play D flat? F sharp? A flat? G minor?

Here's how you figure it out - in case you haven't figured it out already. The capo raises the pitch of the guitar one half-step for each fret.

So, to play in a key you don't know, merely look to the left (down the scale) of the unknown chord until you come to a chord you do know. Then count the number of notes (they're called "half steps") you've skipped and put the capo that many frets up the neck of the guitar. Now finger the familiar chord and there you have it.

So - D flat? Look back one to C. Capo goes on first fret and finger C = D flat.

The Chromatic Scale

The half steps, starting from the low E string, proceed like this:

If you have any doubts as to the morality of the use of the capo here is an article by Jerry Silverman on the subject reprinted from Volume 8, Number 1 (Spring 1958) of Sing Out:

THE CAPO - Guitarists' Boon or Bane?

The capo has had a long and honorable history. The word itself comes from the Italian capotasto, but its origins are much older and more diverse than, let us say, renaissance Italy - the source of so much of our musical terminology. For the uninitiated the capo (pr. kay' po) is a piece of metal or rubber (traditionally, wood or ivory) clamped over the fingerboard of the guitar to raise the pitch of all the strings simultaneously by an equal amount. Representations of different types of capos are to be found on ancient stone carvings of people playing stringed instruments, in paintings of different periods, and mention is made of them in books of instruction dealing with lutes, citterns, guitars, and other stringed instruments.

Despite this long, traditional use the guitarist who uses a capo today is very often the object of ridicule, or, at best, the butt of some sarcastic remark by a well-meaning, but uninformed member of the musical fraternity. A jazz guitarist, who does not use a capo, is apt to say to a folk guitarist who does, "Man, you mean you can't play in F-sharp minor?" A classical guitarist who shudders at the very idea of a capo may not even express his thoughts, but may smile condescendingly as if to say, "Oh well, what's the use - obviously no technique at all." Other musicians refer to the capo as a "crutch" or "cheater".

Even many folk guitarists who use capos and recognize their value have developed guilt feelings brought on by this constant barrage of criticism.

What answers are there to these critics? Are there any answers at all? I believe that there are - and sound musical ones at that.

We must examine the objectives of the folk guitarist as distinguished from those of his jazz and classical colleagues.

The crux of the matter lies in the fact that in most cases the folk guitarist's choice of key will be determined by the vocal range of the performer, a situation only sometimes encountered by the jazzman and never by the classicist. Then, it must be noted that traditional vocal accompaniment demands the legato quality of open-string chords merging and blending with each other rather than the staccato beat of the dance-band guitar. With a dance-band guitarist a capo would get in the way because he purposely avoids playing open strings in order to be able to achieve his desired effect: a steady, clipped beat. Ask him to play, say, Greensleeves, in F-sharp minor and see what happens. He'll play all the right chords but it will come out sounding like The Tennessee Waltz. Ask him to play a flowing accompaniment while his first finger is glued across all the strings at the second fret and you will probably get a pained look. It's not his fault. He may be any excellent guitarist but you just can't do without open strings if you want to have a sustained folk sound.

The classical guitarist is even easier to dispose of. Just ask him in what key he played that Bach prelude. When he tells you, "A major", remind him gently that the original key of the piece was probably B flat and Segovia for whoever made the transcription) - being a realist - transposed the thing to A for ease in playing. This is exactly what the capo does. The difference is that the folk guitarist has the additional problem of vocal range and so he must suit the guitar to the voice and then the fingering (if it comes out in an awkward key) to the guitar. The classical guitarist, with no such vocal problem, merely transposes the piece to the easiest playing key. You don't see the capo when Segovia plays, but it's there all the time.

Flamenco guitarists, whose technical virtuosity is unrivalled by any musicians' - Sabicas, Montoya, Escudero, and the rest - all accompany dancers and singers and, hence, all use capos as a matter of course.

Unquestionably, many less competent folk guitarists do use the capo as a convenient way out of somewhat difficult situations. But the mere use of the capo does not in itself indicate incompetence. There is no substitute for learning to play chords like F-sharp minor and B flat and all the rest. At any moment, in any piece in any key you may be called upon to play a chord involving a barre or a relatively unfamiliar fingering pattern. A capo cannot help you there, but it would be equally foolhardy for a folk guitarist to start a piece in one of these awkward keys. A good guitarist is one who has learned from experience and knows instinctively just when and when not to attach his capo.

ON THE BUYING OF A GUITAR...

Even on this seemingly most basic question there is a variety of opinion. The question is not only one of what brand to acquire and how much to spend but also the seemingly perplexing problem of the nylon-strung (classical) guitar versus the steel-strung flat top guitar. Here are three somewhat concurring, somewhat conflicting and somewhat confusing statements on the subject.

The first is an article which appeared in Volume 1, Number 8 of Sing Out way back in January 1951.

...SO YOU WANNA BUY A GUITAR
An Authoratative Article
by Joe Jaffe

If you want to get a decent instrument, you'll have to buy a new Martin or Gibson* or one of the hand-made Spanish varieties ranging from sixty-five up to a few thousand dollars. If you have the dough, swell - don't read this article: it's intended for the poorer class.

At this point someone tells me skeptically that they've seen good guitars for $5, $10, $15. "Why, they have strings and all, bright colors, and you can comb your hair in the shiny wood." Vehemently I reply that they represent a capitalistic plot to take in a large unsuspecting market. These "guitars" are made of inferior grain, unseasoned wood, sound tinny, would give Frankenstein sore fingers, and their hard, shiny varnish only kills the tone some more.

The solution is to get a second-hand instrument in some pawn shop or old instrument store. I'll tell you how to spot a good one before it falls into the clutches of those hateful enthusiasts who stuff their closets with instruments they never play.

First of all, we want to get the round-hole, flat-top guitar since this type has the most resonant sound. The f-hole variety only sounds good when electrically amplified and is usually found in swing-band playing. Now if you're lucky, you'll find a hand-made "classical" model. These are distinguished by a very wide and thin keyboard, a thin wood face and a characteristic bridge with horizontal string holes. These are the best of guitars and their playing gives real pleasure. Their appearance is usually duller due to the soft varnish used.

Look at the face of your guitar. It should have the close, straight grain of good spruce and is usually light-colored. The back and sides are usually of darker short-grained mahogany, or in the better models, of red-brown richly flowing-grain rosewood.

The keyboard on a good instrument is made of smooth, black ebony, though rosewood is used too. If there are two cut-out channels in the wood of the gear box, this alone will usually denote a good guitar.

The most important thing for beginners is the string action. You can always spot a cheap guitar since you can put your hand in the space between the keyboard and the strings. The strings shouldn't be more than 1/8 inch from the keyboard or terrible blisters and frustration

---

* Since this article was written, several other guitar manufacturers have entered the folk music field, particularly Goya, Guild and Favilla.

will ensue. If the action is bad due to warping, it sometimes pays to straighten out an obviously superior instrument. Action can be improved by filing down the notches on the nut and bridge and by changing the strings to the silk and steel variety.

Good Hunting!

This appeared in the first edition of The Folksinger's Guitar Guide by Pete Seeger.

HOW AND WHERE TO GET A GUITAR

A good new guitar - like any good musical instrument, is expensive. $25 up to several hundred dollars. If you are in a hurry, and can afford it, any music store will be glad to help you spend your money.

For accompanying yourself singing folk songs, steer clear of electric guitars, guitars with "f" holes in the sounding box, instead of a round hole, and instead, select a "Spanish" style guitar. Especially if you have never played a guitar. I'd suggest you start with nylon strings, even if later on you decide you prefer the twang of steel strings. Much easier on the finger-tips.

If you have time to poke around second hand stores, and if you have a guitar playing friend to accompany you, you might get a better buy. Be wary for following points: lay a straight edge (such as a ruler) along the fingerboard to determine if the neck is warped. Cracks can be mended but straightening a warped neck is a major operation, useless to attempt except in the case of an unusually fine instrument worth saving. Se if all the frets are smooth and of even height. If the pegs don't turn easily, it will cost you a few dollars to replace them.

Listen to the tone of several dozen instruments, and you'll be able to tell which please you best. Some are weak in the bass notes, others weak in the high notes. Some are not loud at all, but still have a superlative quiet balance of tone.

When you have it, treat it as you would a violin; keep it dry, and don't put it near too much heat - as on top of a radiator. Remember, one drop on a hard floor will produce a crack expensive to mend. Change the strings when they get to sound too dull, and oil the tuning pegs to make them turn smoothly. (If the guitar has old fashioned wooden friction pegs, that is a separate problem! They're awfully tricky to use.)

· · ·

To complete the trilogy we have part of a "Git Box" article from Volume 7, Number 3 (Fall 1957) of Sing Out by Jerry Silverman:

...SHOULD I BUY A NYLON OR STEEL STRING GUITAR?

This is a problem which generally confronts every prospective folk guitarist - and the choice is often a difficult one to make. Both types of strings have something to be said for and against them.

Nylon strung guitars are usually referred to as "classical" guitars. A classical guitar is distinguishable by its rather wide fingerboard, slotted tuning mechanism, flat top, round sound hole and a bridge with the string holes drilled parallel to the top of the guitar. A classical guitarist invariably uses his bare fingers to pluck the nylon (formerly gut) strings. The quality of the sound produced in this manner is somewhat on the delicate side, although Flamenco guitarists using similar instruments can achieve percussive effects by using their fingernails. Folk guitarists who use the classical guitar are limiting in advance the number of types of folksongs they can successfully attack.

By way of explanation, let us examine the steel string guitar. This guitar should also have a flat top and round sound hole. Its fingerboard is somewhat narrower than that of its classical cousin and the strings are generally attached to the bridge by pegs. This guitar can be played equally well with the bare fingers or with a variety of flat or finger picks. The quality of sound is more incisive and forceful.

Discounting a preference for the sound (timbre), what would make a prospective guitarist choose nylon over steel? After all, anything that can be played on nylon can be played on steel - and then some! Blues, hillbilly, jazz, group-song leading - to name just a few - are some of the areas where a nylon string guitar cannot compete with steel.

The choice is often made for non-musical reasons: Insidious propaganda of the Nylon Trust has brainwashed the gullible populace into believing that steel string guitars are physically more difficult to play and that blood poisoning may occur from pressing down on rusty strings.

Our answer to that is, "Forsooth"! A good guitar is easy to manipulate - steel or nylon. That's the secret. Get as good an instrument as you possibly can afford. There is a false economy in getting a cheap guitar if you are at all serious about studying.

And as far as the blood poisoning is concerned, most of the people recover anyway...

FINGERNAILS

In case you haven't noticed already it's of utmost importance that the fingernails of each hand be the right length.

Those of the left hand will have to be short so the fingers can come down directly and firmly on the string, without the nail touching at all.

← FRETS →

Those on the right hand should be neither too long or too short. When plucking the flesh of the fingertip should touch the string first but the nail be last to leave it.

The following symbols are used in this chart:

P = Primary bass string
A = Alternate bass string
(= Barre

⌒ = Optional barre
x = String not to be played
○ = Open string to be played

The number to the right of some of the diagrams indicates the fret at which the chord is to begin. The chord patterns given here present only one possible fingering for each chord. However, all of the barre chord patterns may be played at any fret (with one half-step change in pitch per fret) thus producing alternate fingerings for all the chords.

	Major	Minor	Dominant 7th	Minor 7th	Added 6th	Major 7th	Minor 6th	Diminished 7th	Augmented	Augmented 7th	Dominant 9th	Dominant 7th with flat 5th
A♭ (G#)	A♭	A♭m	A♭7	A♭m7	A♭6	A♭M7	A♭m6	A♭°	A+	A♭+7	A♭9	A♭7♭5
A	A	Am	A7	Am7	A6	AM7	Am6	A°	A+	A+7	A9	A7♭5
B♭	B♭	B♭m	B♭7	B♭m7	B♭6	B♭M7	B♭m6	B♭°	B+	B♭+7	B♭9	B♭7♭5
B	B	Bm	B7	Bm7	B6	BM7	Bm6	B°	B+	B+7	B9	B7♭5
C	C	Cm	C7	Cm7	C6	CM7	Cm6	C°	C+	C+7	C9	C7♭5
C# (D♭)	C#	C#m	C#7	C#m7	C#6	C#M7	C#m6	C#°	C#+	C#+7	C#9	C#7♭5
D	D	Dm	D7	Dm7	D6	DM7	Dm6	D°	D+	D+7	D9	D7♭5
E♭	E♭	E♭m	E♭7	E♭m7	E♭6	E♭M7	E♭m6	E°	E♭+	E♭+7	E♭9	E♭7♭5
E	E	Em	E7	Em7	E6	EM7	Em6	E°	E+	E+7	E9	E7♭5
F	F	Fm	F7	Fm7	F6	FM7	Fm6	F°	F+	F+7	F9	F7♭5
F# (G♭)	F#	F#m	F#7	F#m7	F#6	F#M7	F#m6	F#°	F#+	F#+7	F#9	F#7♭5
G	G	Gm	G7	Gm7	G6	GM7	Gm6	G°	G+	G+7	G9	G7♭5

(F, Major) if played with barre hold at 1st fret